CHEYENNE'S
CAPITOL
AVENUE
BRONZE

HISTORY ENSHRINED

STARLEY TALBOTT AND
MICHAEL E. KASSEL

Foreword by
Cheyenne Mayor Patrick Collins

THE
History
PRESS

Published by The History Press
Charleston, SC
www.historypress.com

Front cover, top left: Former Wyoming governors (*from left*, Francis E. Warren, Nellie Tayloe Ross, Robert Carey and John Kendrick), circa 1925; *top right*: former governor Nellie Tayloe Ross in front of the Wyoming Capitol; *center left*: George Rainsford, Cheyenne architect; *center right*: Chief Washakie, ancestral leader; *bottom left*: *Sheep Wagon*, honoring agriculture; *bottom right*: former United States Supreme Court justice Willis Van Devanter.

Back cover, top left: Former governor Francis E. Warren in front of the Wyoming Capitol; *top right*: *Comparing Time*, honoring the railroad; *center left*: Joseph Stimson, photographer; *bottom left*: *Hard to Leave*, a cowboy in front of the Historic Railroad Depot.

First published 2024

Manufactured in the United States

ISBN 9781467157612

Library of Congress Control Number: 2024931864

CONTENTS

CONTENTS

FOREWORD

When I travel, I often see other cities' glories—their vibrant parks, their distinctive architecture and art, all the things that make them special—and ask myself, "How did this come to be? What or who was the spark that made this a reality?" This book is important because it tells the story of several tipping points in the Capitol Avenue Bronze Project—those moments when an idea conceived more than a decade earlier finally took actionable shape, inspired a handful of private citizens committed to preserving the history of the state and very rapidly grew into the most successful public arts project in Cheyenne history.

The story within the story is how the project grew very rapidly from an idea that had long languished into an overnight success, as things go. As you will read in these pages, the idea was modest at first. In 2010, Harvey Deselms, a local art dealer who hails from a longtime Wyoming ranching family, had the idea of raising funds to install bronze statues on 17th Street in Cheyenne. His idea later focused on Capitol Avenue rather than 17th Street. Capitol Avenue is the historic street that runs from the Union Pacific Railroad Train Depot, a focal point of downtown tourism, on the south end of the street and travels north seven blocks to the capitol building, the terminus of nonresidential Capitol Avenue. In the eleven years between 2010 and 2021, Harvey was successful in raising funds to install three statues, which helped keep the project alive.

Another turning point came in late summer 2021, when another man with deep Wyoming roots, Nathaniel Trelease, was talking to Harvey about a simple framing project that Harvey had done for him. In that moment, Nathaniel told Harvey that he was looking for a legacy project for his family to honor his mother who had passed away in August of that year. When Harvey reminded Nathaniel of the bronze statue idea, the idea captured his imagination.

In October 2021, I met with the two men at the Paramount Café in Cheyenne and walked Capitol Avenue on a cool fall morning. Nathaniel presented his ideas for how the project should be reorganized and led by a handful of private citizens with a commitment to preserving the state's history. No public funds would be used. Donations would not be sought. Rather, donors would be asked to donate statues. And most importantly, the project would focus on the state's history, the iconic people of our history—the explorers and settlers, the planters and ranchers, the statesmen and women, the lawmen, military heroes, novelists and architects—whom everyone, resident and visitor alike, should know more about.

I was inspired. I had an early taste of wanting a share in what should have been done long ago—telling the story of one of only fifty states. Before I left that meeting, I appointed Nathaniel as chairman of the commission and Harvey as curator of the Capitol Avenue Bronze Commission. Nathaniel soon recruited a small group of private citizens with long-standing ties to Wyoming and a commitment to preserving its heritage—Dixie Roberts, Caren Murray, Susan Samuelson and Jeff Wallace—to join the commission.

Six people and an idea. That is how this civic project began. The commission originally hoped to install statues on the twenty-five corners of Capitol Avenue that did not have a statue yet. I was skeptical that the seemingly audacious plan that had long stalled could be completed even in many years. But you could tell in the very early going that the impulse to preserve the state's history was latent in many people, for when the commission members started telling the story of this rare, multi-generational opportunity to tell the story of one of the fifty states, dozens of donors—individuals and families—quickly emerged to support the project and donate commissioned statues of Wyoming figures.

It only took twenty months from October 2021 for the commission to install twenty-five statues on all the street corners on Capitol Avenue. Since that time, the project has grown so rapidly that the commission has installed more than twenty statues on 17th Street, fulfilling Harvey's original idea, as well as on nearby Carey, Warren, Central and Pioneer Streets.

Wyoming is America's smallest state by population (578,000 statewide at this writing) though one of the largest by size (nearly 100,000 square miles), and its story is often reduced to the cliché of cowboys and Indians in the Old West. Because of the generous donations of dozens of statue donors, the bronze project is a corrective, visually telling the history of the city and state in public art, engaging the more than 1 million people who visit Cheyenne every year and telling a more layered, complete and rich history of a people who have made contributions to law, architecture, literature, politics and the military.

Wyoming is the Equality State. But of those more than 1 million visitors to Cheyenne every year, very few know that America's first female judge, Esther Hobart Morris, was working in Wyoming and lived near Capitol Avenue in Cheyenne. A few more know that America's first elected female governor, Nellie Tayloe Ross, was elected in Wyoming. But virtually none know the role of Therese Alberta Jenkins of Cheyenne in saving Wyoming's suffrage in the state.

Similarly, few may know that Cheyenne has a storied part of America's Gilded Age. Cattle barons from England mixed with New York City financiers and socialites in the streets and residential parlors of Cheyenne, often at the grand Cheyenne Club. Many of the public buildings and residences in this part of Cheyenne were designed by George Rainsford, a New York architect who designed some of the most distinctive and varied homes and buildings in Cheyenne, some of which remain standing in a historic district that bears his name.

Others may know Cheyenne's Warren Air Force Base but not know that it's named after Francis E. Warren, Wyoming's last territorial governor, first state governor and longest-serving U.S. senator who was, in his time, a lion of the Senate and something of a pioneer, appointing the first woman to head the staff of a Senate Committee and the first African American committee clerk.

All of these and many other men and women are represented in bronze statues in Cheyenne, Wyoming. But there will be no more "spoilers" here. Thanks to Starley Talbott and Michael Kassel, the authors of this book, you'll learn more about them and many others who are part of the Capitol Avenue Bronze Project. When people carve their own or a loved one's name into a tree stump during a hike or on an upright stone in a cemetery or leave their name on a bronze plaque attached to a statue, the impulse throughout time is always the same: they aspire for someone or something to be remembered.

As the fifty-seventh mayor of Cheyenne, a position once held by Governor and Senator Francis E. Warren, I am extremely proud to have held this office when this project was renewed and grew into such a grand success. I am grateful to the Capitol Avenue Bronze Commission's steward, Harvey Deselms, for his tenacity and to Starley Talbott and Michael Kassel for writing this book. May our common work inspire many generations of Cheyenne and Wyoming to come.

—Patrick Collins,
Mayor, Cheyenne, October 2023

ACKNOWLEDGEMENTS

The authors are grateful for the many people who made the compilation of this book a reality. Without the writing, research and assistance of many historians, we could not have written this narrative.

Special thanks go to the staff and volunteers at the Wyoming State Archives, especially Suzi Taylor and Robin Everett.

A very special thank-you goes to Cheyenne mayor Patrick Collins for writing the foreword for our book and for his dedication to the bronze legacy project.

We are grateful for the vision and leadership of Harvey Deselms, who never gave up on his dream for public art in Cheyenne, and to Nathaniel Trelease, who added the spark to make the dream come true. The commission members—Dixie Roberts, Caren Murray, Susan Samuelson and Jeff Wallace—provided advice and support for the project.

It has been a great privilege to meet the sculptors who used their artistic talents in creating the statues that fill Capitol Avenue and beyond with their interpretations of people and objects that add to the history of Wyoming. Special thanks to Joey Bainer for a tour of the Art Castings foundry in Loveland, Colorado.

In addition to the sculptors, thanks go to the people who provided the support for each statue. Don Jones, master mason, created the stone pedestals holding each sculpture and spent hours setting the statues in place. Jake Johnson, president of Harold F. Johnson Masonry, provided transport of the sculptures to each site and assistance in setting them in place.

Our great appreciation goes to the folks who donated a sculpture to add to the legacy of Cheyenne. It has been an inspiration to conduct interviews with many of these donors. We also give special thanks to several people who provided information about their families.

Special thanks to our acquisitions editor, Artie Crisp, and others at The History Press for their support and guidance.

Most importantly, we are grateful for our families and our spouses. Michael thanks his wife, Amy, who has been the wind beneath his wings, blessing him with her encouragement and fortitude. Starley thanks her husband, Beauford Thompson, for his support in so many ways.

Starley thanks her coauthor, Michael Kassel, for his important research and for his speaking ability, which first inspired her to delve further into the fascinating history of Cheyenne. Michael wishes to thank Starley Talbott for inspiring him to put into print that which inspired him about the people of Cheyenne and for opening doors he didn't think possible.

Lastly, we thank our readers and the many people who continue to inspire us with a love of history.

INTRODUCTION

The history of Cheyenne can be told through its buildings and monuments. Every great cultural capital of the world has one or many streets that inspire residents and visitors to learn more about the area. The purpose of the Capitol Avenue Bronze Legacy Project is to inspire learning about the history of Wyoming.

Cheyenne's history has had a major impact on the growth of our nation, not just the state of Wyoming. Every aspect of the city and state's story is meant to honor and recognize the area's contribution to arts, science, law, architecture, military, wildlife, agriculture, the Native population and more.

The goals of the Capitol Avenue Bronze Legacy Project include paying tribute to the pioneering spirit of the people of the state, providing a permanent example of the dignity of classic art in public places and featuring historic figures and scenes from everyday life.

The project is a multi-generational opportunity to honor the city and state and pay tribute to an individual or family. Every statue has been donated by an individual or a group. Each sculpture is mounted on a stone pedestal that was crafted by a local stonemason. The pedestal contains a plaque stating the name of the artist and the donor, including the person or family to whom it pays tribute. Many of the bronze statues also display QR codes.

The story of Cheyenne's bronze sculptures is an ongoing one. Once the statues began gracing corners along Capitol Avenue, more of the city's residents stepped up to donate a sculpture that was important to their family values. Some groups were formed to enable folks to contribute to a sculpture when they were unable to provide one on a personal basis. After Capitol Avenue was filled from the capitol to the historic Railroad Depot, statues soon began to appear on other streets.

Previously, a few statues were scattered throughout Cheyenne and on the grounds of the state capitol. However, there had never been a concerted effort to provide a continuous flow of sites telling the story of the city and the state.

What began as a dream became an ongoing story. The story is not finished. Within each statue along Capitol Avenue and other streets were placed time capsules. Perhaps future generations will also be inspired when they may open these time capsules.

This book includes the story behind each sculpture, along with profiles of the dreamers who kindled the idea and narratives of the artists and the donors. It is the authors' hope that residents and visitors will explore the avenues and streets of Cheyenne to marvel at the monuments created to preserve the history and heritage of Wyoming.

PART I

THE DREAMERS

HARVEY DESELMS, CURATOR

Some dreams come to life in unexpected ways. For more than a decade, Harvey Deselms dreamed of placing statues of animals along 17th Street in Cheyenne, beginning with statues in front of his art gallery on the corner of House Avenue and 17th Street.

Harvey's dream was nearly dormant for many years despite his constant "bugging of some folks around Cheyenne," he said. In 2010, with the support of Leadership Cheyenne, a program of the chamber of commerce to foster community leadership, that year's class sponsored a sculpture of a cowboy on the southeast corner of Capitol Avenue and Lincolnway. The statue, called *Duster*, was a symbol of the cowboy state of Wyoming. A few other statues were then scattered along Capitol Avenue, years before the dedication of the completion of a sculpture on every corner of Capitol Avenue from the state capitol to the historic train depot.

Deselms grew up on the family ranch at Albin, Wyoming. His love of art was ingrained as a child when he found rocks on the ranch, many of which included Native artifacts. He also learned the value of contributing in the small and close-knit community of Albin. "Everyone helped out on the ranch and in the community," Harvey said.

As a graduate of Albin High School and with an associate degree in archaeology and anthropology from Laramie County Community College, Deselms went on to become the assistant director of the Old West Museum

Harvey Deselms, curator of the bronze project, displaying a sign presented by the Cheyenne Chamber of Commerce for the Business Beautification Award to the Capitol Avenue Bronze Commission and Deselms Fine Art Gallery for the downtown bronze installations. *Starley Talbott photograph.*

in Cheyenne. He learned about art through his work at the museum and eventually left his position there in 1992 to establish his art gallery. He considers the Old West Museum to be one of the most wonderful aspects of Cheyenne and continues to serve on the board of directors.

Eventually housing his large collection of art featuring artists from Wyoming and neighboring states, Deselms Fine Art Gallery was established in the historic Union Pacific Railroad's house for the company doctor at 303 East 17th Street.

In 2020, Harvey Deselms received the Wyoming Tribune Eagle Community Spirit Award. The award was a tribute to his longtime involvement in service throughout Cheyenne, including the Cheyenne Animal Shelter, Comea Shelter, Cheyenne Regional Medical Center, Boys & Girls Club and the Cheyenne Frontier Days™ Old West Museum art shows. Deselms was nominated for the award by Karen and Dean "Doc" Schroeder. Doc Schroeder described Harvey: "He is genuine. What you see is what you get with Harvey. He's got a great sense of humor, he's a funny guy and he's not putting that on for anybody. He exudes humanity and is a people person."

However, in the back of Harvey Deselms's mind was his dream of installing bronze sculptures on the streets of Cheyenne. A visit from local resident, Nathaniel Trelease, to the art gallery provided the spark that ignited the Capitol Avenue Bronze Project. Trelease admired several of the bronze sculptures on display at the gallery, and several conversations with Deselms during the following days led to the establishment of a commission to support the project. With the endorsement of Mayor Patrick Collins, a commission was appointed, and the sparks began to fly.

Deselms contacted several local and regional artists to see if they were interested in providing sculptures for the project. Donors were elicited from the community to provide the funds for acquiring the desired historical sculptures. The first installation of the revitalized dream was placed in October 2021—a sculpture named *In Good Hands* by Robin Laws, donated by Nathaniel Trelease in memory of his mother.

On dedication day, June 10, 2023, Capitol Avenue was adorned with thirty-five bronze sculptures, on every corner of the avenue from the Wyoming Capitol to the historic Union Pacific Railroad Depot. Every statue had been donated by private donors, costing the taxpayers of the city nothing. Mayor Patrick Collins welcomed the crowd to the momentous event. The Cheyenne League of Voters provided educational interpreters for many of the historical statues.

Harvey's dream lives on and continues to grow. The project will continue beyond Capitol Avenue for the installation of public art along the streets and avenues of Cheyenne.

Nathaniel Trelease, Board Chairman

Clouds formed around the dome of the Wyoming Capitol while crowds gathered in front of the building for the Capitol Avenue Bronze dedication ceremony on June 10, 2023. Following the welcome by Cheyenne mayor Patrick Collins, Nathaniel Trelease presented a summary of the achievements of the community in completing the placement of historical bronze sculptures on Capitol Avenue.

Less than two years earlier, the dream of placing sculptures along Cheyenne's premier avenue had languished like fading embers of a campfire.

Mayor Patrick Collins welcomed attendees to the bronze dedication ceremony. *Starley Talbott photograph.*

At just the right moment, the embers were reignited when Nathaniel Trelease walked into Deselms Fine Art Gallery looking for a way to honor his mother following her death. Nathaniel and Harvey Deselms, owner of the gallery, spoke about Harvey's long-held dream for bronze sculptures to grace the streets and avenues of Cheyenne. Their conversation led to a meeting with Cheyenne's mayor and the formation of the Capitol Avenue Bronze Commission.

As the chairman of the bronze project, Trelease's vision for the success of the mission included the idea that it should be approached from the perspective that every great cultural capital of the world has one or many streets that inspire people to learn more about the place.

"In Washington, D.C., it's the Mall east of the United States Capitol, with its monuments and memorials to Washington, Lincoln, heroic sacrifice and valor in war and its tribute to all of the states. In Rome and London, there are many streets near the great basilicas and Houses of Parliament. In Cheyenne, that street is Capitol Avenue," said Trelease.

The Capitol Avenue Bronze Commission members—including Jeff Wallace, Dixie Roberts, Caren Murray and Susan Samuelson—agreed

Left: Nathaniel Trelease, chairman of the bronze project, spoke at the dedication ceremony. *Starley Talbott photograph.*

Below: The Capitol Avenue Bronze Commission members. *From left*: Jeff Wallace, Dixie Roberts, Susan Samuelson, Caren Murray and Harvey Deselms, curator. *Starley Talbott photograph.*

that the project should embrace every aspect of the city and state's story, representing not only the explorers, settlers, lawmen and great women of the state but also the city and the state's contributions to the fields of arts and letters, law and architecture, as well as recognition of its military heroes. The commission also expressed the desire to honor the state's Native population and recognize the importance of wildlife and livestock to the state.

The original plan for the project was to secure donations for twenty-eight statues to fill Capitol Avenue from the capitol to the historic railroad depot. The hope was for individuals, families, churches and businesses to be inspired to tell the story of Wyoming by contributing to the project. As the story spread, many traditional and new donors were excited to participate in the legacy.

The first new sculpture installation happened in October 2021 on Capitol Avenue and 21st Street. Nathaniel Trelease donated the sculpture created by Robin Laws, named *In Good Hands*, in honor of his mother.

Soon the map of Capitol Avenue began to be filled with the names of donors and the sculptures they wanted to contribute. Each new statue was recognized with an installation ceremony at its designated place along the avenue.

Each sculpture was placed on a stone pedestal built by Don Jones, a Wyoming native and fifth-generation mason. Jones and Jack Johnson, owner of H.F. Johnson Masonry, were on site for every installation.

By June 2023, every corner of Capitol Avenue from the capitol to the historic Railroad Depot contained a bronze sculpture honoring the legacy of the city and the state. The last statue to be installed near the capitol was the one honoring Nellie Tayloe Ross, the first female governor of Wyoming and the nation.

Additional donors were inspired to embrace the concept of placing sculptures along several other streets in Cheyenne, including 17th Street, Carey Avenue, Pioneer Avenue and others. Commitments came in for statues of animals to fulfill Deselms's early vision of a corridor of animals on 17th Street.

Nathaniel Trelease summed up the story with these words: "Something remarkable happened in Cheyenne from October 2021 to June 2023. What began as a dream became a story, and the story became a plan and the plan was fulfilled. It is a tribute to many, all of whom were inspired to preserve the history and heritage of the state and be an example to the nation of Wyoming pride."

PART II
THE ARTISTS

Guadalupe Barajas, Sculptor

Artist Guadalupe Barajas has been a remarkably creative force on the Cheyenne arts scene for many years. His sculptures grace many locations throughout our community, capturing the majesty of Wyoming's natural environment and the people who make it their home.

Barajas was born on the Wind River Indian Reservation near Riverton, Wyoming, where his grandmother was serving as a midwife in 1943. He and his family moved to Cheyenne, where he grew up and eventually graduated from the first class of East High School in 1961.

Barajas moved to Chicago, where he attended the School of the Art Institute of Chicago, receiving his Bachelor of Fine Arts degree in three-dimensional design. He remained in the Chicago area as an art teacher with the Chicago Public School System, eventually working at Paul Robeson High School. He married his spouse and raised his family in Chicago. His teaching career of twenty-six years was capped with his receipt of the Golden Apple Award for Excellence in Teaching in March 1992. Utilizing the $2,500 he earned as a stipend, Barajas took a sabbatical, during which he rediscovered his true calling as a sculptor.

After retiring from teaching, Barajas returned to Cheyenne and began his life as a professional sculptor in earnest in 1994. Initially, Guadalupe focused primarily on wildlife. As time progressed, he also began sculpting depictions

Guadalupe Barajas with his *Sky Messenger* statue. *Starley Talbott photograph.*

of Indigenous peoples, gravitating toward his own heritage and its place in our society.

Bronze art from Barajas's studio began appearing in galleries and public spaces across the country. Ranging in size from the smallest animal bust to larger-than-life monuments, his work is regularly featured in western art shows around the nation. His depictions of wildlife have earned him many awards from art and conservation groups and appear in Cheyenne at the Wyoming Game and Fish Department, Sierra Trading Post and Laramie County Community College, as well as in several of Cheyenne's city parks. He is most proud of *Open Season*, his thirteen-foot-high depiction of three mule deer in flight that was chosen to sit in front of the Wyoming Governor's Mansion by Governor Dave Freudenthal.

When asked to participate in the Capitol Avenue Bronze Project, Barajas was primed to begin. The first subject he was asked to sculpt was Cheyenne's founder, Grenville M. Dodge. He had been considering a similar project for years, trying to enlist many patrons to erect a monument to the man near Cheyenne's depot to no avail. It was with great satisfaction that Barajas saw the statue of Dodge erected at the corner of Capitol Avenue and 16th Street near the historic railroad depot. Other Capitol Avenue statues created by Barajas include *Family Barbers Legacy* and works depicting Francis E. Warren and Chief Washakie.

Barajas and his wife, Elsie, enjoy a comfortable life in Cheyenne, living in their combined home and studio where many of his paintings and bronze sculptures pay tribute to his artistic talent. He is known affectionately by his many friends as "Lupe," and he summed up his work with these words:

> *Unless one has seriously sculpted, it would seem difficult understanding the feeling of literally taking a lump of clay and breathing life into it. This is my reality as a bronze sculptor. Unlike painting, where I've created illusions of space, sculpture consumes its space as it takes on a life of its own. Every angle of its composition presents a new perspective and an added challenge to my creative energy. Sculpting, for me is truly an intimate experience. Capturing that inner spirit and energy of one's subject involves an intimate connection. That is what separates mediocrity from the real deal.*

Joel Turner, Sculptor

Two adjectives that describe Joel Turner are *talented* and *tenacious*. Turner has lived most of his life in Loveland, Colorado, where he now owns his own art studio and specializes in sculpture.

Turner was always interested in art, and he expressed that interest through drawing while in high school. However, he did not see art as a way to provide an income. He learned to be a welder at a community college and found work at a fabrication shop for a few months. Turner still yearned to apply his skills as an artist and tried to make a small sculpture, but he was not very successful at first, he says.

Through a family friendship and visits to the Lundeen farm, where Joel's father shoed horses, Joel found an opportunity to succeed as an artist. He learned that George Lundeen was planning to hire a welder for his sculpture studio in Loveland. Joel won the job and began a nine-year career as a welder for the Lundeen Studios.

Lundeen Studios was established by George Lundeen in 1976 in Loveland, Colorado. His works include sculptures from tabletop size to large monuments. The sculptures are found in collections throughout the world, including Denver International Airport; Statuary Hall in Washington, D.C.; universities; and many other locations.

During his time as a welder, Turner learned the skills necessary to create a sculpture, including mold making, production, waxwork, metal chasing and patina. At the Lundeen studio, Joel became involved with many sculptural projects of significance, including the Stations of the Cross, commissioned for the Cloisters on the Platte Foundation in Nebraska; a fiftieth-anniversary commemoration for the Apollo 11 crew, installed at the Kennedy Space Center; and many other projects.

Turner's tenacious spirit led him to establish his own sculpture business in 2021 and become the owner of his art studio in Loveland in 2022. Joel's talent was discovered by Harvey Deselms, the curator of the Capitol Avenue Sculpture Project, when he was finding artists to provide the sculptures. Joel and Harvey soon began collaborating on plans for several sculptures. By the time the dedication of the Capitol Avenue bronze statues occurred on June 10, 2023, Turner had created nine of the thirty-five statues on Cheyenne's Capitol Avenue.

The Turner sculptures for Capitol Avenue include historical depictions of Nellie Tayloe Ross, Willis Vandevanter, Esther Hobart Morris, Therese Jenkins, Mary O'Hara, George Rainsford, Joseph Stimson and Admiral Jake McInerney, along with a community-based work called *Working Together for Others*.

Each sculpture involves extensive research in the time period of each historical figure, including the clothing fashion of the period. Some sculptures are based on photographs of the person or family members. Joel explained the process of creating a sculpture including these elements by using the "lost wax" method: creating a sketch; sculpting a clay mold; adding rubber paint to the mold; adding wax to the mold; casting by pouring molten bronze into the mold; cooling the metal that is cut into pieces; welding the sculpture pieces together after casting; grinding, polishing and buffing the metal; and applying a patina to finish the sculpture.

Since the sculptures for the Capitol Avenue project are not full size and are displayed outside, Joel has added innovations to some of the statues. He explained that smaller sculptures displayed outside are harder to see when finished in traditional bronze tones. Joel began experimenting with adding color to the patina. The sculptures of Nellie Tayloe Ross, George Rainsford and Jake McInerney have a color patina.

Turner's favorite sculpture on Capitol Avenue, and the one he fashioned in his own image, is that of famed photographer of the West Joseph Stimson.

Joel Turner, *left*, with his clay mold of Therese Jenkins, *center*, and Paula Qualls, great-granddaughter of Therese Jenkins. *Starley Talbott photograph.*

He is also very proud of the final statue installed near the state capitol of Nellie Tayloe Ross, clad in a blue dress. Ross was elected in 1924 as the first female governor in Wyoming and the United States of America.

Another sculpture of great historic significance in Wyoming created by Turner is that of Therese Jenkins. Jenkins was an advocate of women's voting rights and the featured speaker during Wyoming's celebration of statehood in 1890. Jenkins's great-granddaughter Paula Qualls lives in Cheyenne. Paula was delighted to visit with Joel in Loveland and admire the clay mold of her great-grandmother.

Turner has also completed work for private collectors, as well as public installations for cities, organizations and businesses. His work will include additional statues in Cheyenne in several locations. Joel spends extensive amounts of time outdoors and is an avid climber. He enjoys visiting with people and exploring literature, where he finds inspiration to express his ideas and talents.

George Lundeen, Sculptor

With hundreds of sculptures scattered throughout the world, George Lundeen could aptly be called the "Dean of Sculpture," at least to those who know him and have viewed his realistic images that capture the human spirit.

Lundeen established Lundeen Studios in Loveland, Colorado, in 1976. Before establishing his studio in Loveland, Lundeen spent a good deal of his time in Nebraska, and he also traveled throughout the world. George was born and raised in Holdrege, Nebraska. He received a Bachelor of Arts degree from Hastings College and a Master of Fine Arts degree from the University of Illinois.

As the recipient of a Fulbright-Hays scholarship, Lundeen spent a year in Florence, Italy. There he studied the work of the old masters of art and was inspired to become a sculptor. Upon returning to Nebraska, however, Lundeen spent several years as a teacher. He taught at the University of Nebraska–Kearney, the University of Illinois and Texas A&M University. Later, he taught classes at the Scottsdale Artist School and the Loveland Academy. He was awarded an honorary Doctor of Humane Letters degree from the University of Nebraska in 1999.

Lundeen moved to Loveland in 1975 and worked at the Arts Casting Foundry for a time. There he learned the process of producing a sculpture that he uses in his own studio. Lundeen Studios molds its original clay sculpture, pours and chases the wax replicas and, when returned from the local foundries, welds, metal chases and patinas the bronze to completion. He was joined in the studio by his brother, Mark, in 1981. Several family members are also involved with the studio today.

Lundeen sculptures are on display from Loveland, Colorado, to Nebraska, Florida, Texas, Illinois, New York, Washington, D.C., and Cheyenne, Wyoming. George said that he has fond memories of attending the Western Spirit Art Show in Cheyenne from the early 1980s to today. "I have met lots of wonderful people in Cheyenne and I have numerous clients there," he said.

A few of Lundeen's most well-known interpretive sculptures include Amelia Earhart in Statuary Hall in the U.S. Capitol; *Crew of Apollo XIII* at the Space Center in Houston, Texas; *The Eagle Has Landed: Crew of Apollo XI*, at the Kennedy Space Center, Florida; Abraham Lincoln at the Presidential Library, Springfield, Illinois; aviator Elrey B. Jeppesen at Denver International Airport; Mighty Casey at the Baseball Hall of Fame in Cooperstown, New York; and several sculptures at Benson Sculpture Park in Loveland, Colorado.

George Lundeen at his Loveland, Colorado studio with a clay mold of *Ribbons and Robins*, a new sculpture. *Starley Talbott photograph.*

The annual Sculpture in the Park exhibition, held each summer in Loveland, is one of George Lundeen's favorite places to greet visitors from all over the world. Known by friends and acquaintances alike, George is a charismatic person who greets people as if he has known them for years and is happy to discuss his favorite subject, sculpture.

The Capitol Avenue bronze sculpture project in Cheyenne is graced with four of George Lundeen's sculptures: *Aviator, Native Girl, Promise of the Prairie* and *Rarin' to Ride*.

Aviator is a smaller replica of the statue of Elrey Jeppesen at the Denver International Airport. Lundeen was a friend of Jeppesen, who was one of the early airmail pilots and established a business in Denver producing aviation maps.

Native Girl is a replica of a small portion of the sculpture *On the Trail of Discovery* at the Great Plains Art Museum, Lincoln, Nebraska. The statue in Cheyenne represents a Native girl who may have been one of the many Natives encountered by Lewis and Clark during their Corps of Discovery journey. Lundeen said that his research shows that the members of the corps often presented gifts to people they met along the way, and the young girl depicted holding a flag may have been presented the flag as a gift.

Promise of the Prairie is part of a bronze display in Lundeen's hometown of Holdrege, Nebraska, representing the pioneer farm families who settled in the area.

Rarin' to Ride depicts a young cowboy holding a saddle who may be eager to saddle up and join the cowboys celebrating Frontier Days™ in Cheyenne. Lundeen is a friend of Dennis Wallace, who donated the statue.

George Lundeen served as a mentor or as an inspiration to many of the sculpture artists whose statues are represented as part of the Capitol Avenue Bronze Legacy of Cheyenne.

JULIE JONES-DENKERS, SCULPTOR

Sculptures exhibiting the values of humanity, joy, an uplifting spirit and whimsy are part of the artistic work of Julie Jones-Denkers. The Loveland, Colorado artist has believed in the value of being a visual and hands-on learner since childhood. "There wasn't a scrap of paper in our household when I was a child that wasn't covered with my drawings," Julie said. She also learned to value nature, gardening and animals during her formative years.

Jones grew up in Loveland and graduated from Loveland High School, where she was the recipient of the Howard Reed Award as an outstanding student, citizen and athlete. She was a two-time state champion and state record holder in track. Julie went on to attend Brigham Young University in Utah, where she competed on the track team and was named the Most Outstanding Female Senior Athlete.

Julie earned a Bachelor of Fine Arts degree from BYU in 1986. Among her many art classes at the university, she took a ceramics class that piqued her interest in sculpture, especially when the instructor told Julie that she should become a sculptor.

During the intervening years, Julie married and became the mother of five children. She lived in Indianapolis for eight years and eventually relocated back to Loveland. She said that she often created sculptures while working in her bedroom, where she could find time to express herself. Julie enjoys creating playful, spontaneous images within her many sculptures. She is especially fond of creating sculptures of women and animals.

As a cancer survivor, Jones-Denkers has often created memorial work for private families. The sculpture that was chosen by John Lee and family for inclusion in the Capitol Avenue Bronze Legacy of Cheyenne serves as

Julie Jones-Denkers with a clay mold of *Life Is Wonderful*, her current work. *Starley Talbott photograph.*

a memorial for Lee's wife, Jackie. The statue, titled *Garden Angel*, is a tribute to all aspects of creation and a reminder that every garden needs an angel, according to Jones-Denkers.

At one point in Julie's art career, she was told that she would never "make it as a sculptor." She didn't believe that for a moment, and she believed that any woman could do anything she put her mind to do. One of her favorite statues is titled *Girls Can Do Anything*. The sculpture depicts a young girl riding a pig and was purchased for display by the Horse Ranch Hotel near Indianapolis.

Jones-Denkers has exhibited her art in many places, including Colorado, Arizona, South Dakota, Minnesota, Kansas and Wyoming. She is the recipient of many sculpture awards, including for *The Conductor*, a People's Choice Award at the Celebration of Color Art Show in Fort Collins, Colorado; *Reading Magic*, a People's Choice Award for Sculptures in the Streets, Mesa, Arizona; *Girls Can Do Anything*, a People's Choice Award, Sculpture Walk, Sioux Falls, South Dakota; and *Don't Play with Your Food*, People's Choice Awards in Evergreen, Colorado, and Sioux Falls, South Dakota. Julie is also a Loveland High School Hall of Fame inductee, honoring people who have demonstrated achievements beyond their high school experiences and excelled in areas of art, community, drama, music, science and sports.

Jones-Denkers currently resides in Fort Collins, Colorado, where she continues to express her life's values in her sculpture work. At one time in her artistic journey, she purchased a welder and completed much of the finishing touches of a statue after it had been cast at the foundry. She said that she became a better sculptor after she learned of the many steps it takes to complete a bronze sculpture.

One of Julie's favorite miniature sculptures that she's often sold at many exhibitions is titled *Life Is Wonderful*. She is currently working on a similar but larger piece depicting the life she lives and believes is "wonderful."

BOBBIE CARLYLE, SCULPTOR

As a sculpture artist, Bobbie Carlyle lives life to the fullest and sees every situation as a positive experience. Her work inspires the viewer to consider the multiple layers of meaning within a sculpture.

The Loveland, Colorado artist received a Bachelor of Fine Arts degree from Brigham Young University in Utah. She has taught numerous workshops, including at the Colorado Institute of Art.

Carlyle has created some of the most compelling figurative work in the art world today. Her work deals with the full spectrum, the complexity of emotion, struggles and triumphs of life. Carlyle says that her own life struggles along with her seven children have been an inspiration to many of her creations.

Among Carlyle's many creations, she is known internationally and recognized for her sculpture titled *Self Made Man*. Many of her other works include figurative children, figurative animals, liturgical pieces, fountains, wildlife, western scenes, tributes to flight and other historical subjects.

Bobbie Carlyle with her statue depicting her son when he was eight years old. *Starley Talbott photograph.*

Carlyle's monuments can be seen throughout Cheyenne, including the three statues she created for the Capitol Avenue Bronze Project. Her sculptures on Capitol Avenue include *Priority Mail, Duster* and *Hard to Leave*.

One of Bobbie's most compelling statues may be found near the entrance to Deselms Fine Art Gallery on 17th Street in Cheyenne. The small sculpture depicts her son at the age of eight trying to capture a frog, titled *I Got Ya*. She said that he was patient enough to spend two forty-five-minute sessions posing for his mother to create the tender sculpture.

"I create monumental bronze sculptures that capture bold strength and provocative intelligence. My work reflects my love for classic sculpture, while presenting a modern approach with its presentation and a psychological approach for connection to the struggles and triumph of life," said Carlyle of her work.

CHRIS NAVARRO, SCULPTOR

Chris Navarro didn't know what he wanted to be when he grew up, but he knew he liked horses. Born into a military family, Chris knew several homes, as his father moved from post to post with the U.S. Air Force.

When he was eleven, Chris was first exposed to horses in Ohio when his father was stationed at Wright-Patterson Air Force Base outside Dayton. A friend's family had several ponies, and Chris remembered spending every moment he could there. He did not have a saddle, but that didn't stop him from riding ponies on many childhood adventures. When his friend's family transferred to a new station, they gave him his first horse, a four-year-old Welsh stallion.

With his first horse, Navarro absorbed knowledge about its habits, emotions and personality. Chris worked at a local stable in exchange for boarding his horse there. He met and befriended the owner of the stable, Bob Joseph, and a professional horse trainer Larry Edwards. The two men furthered Chris's education about horses, and using what he learned, Chris began showing his horses at local 4-H fairs and started winning awards by the age of fifteen. However, Chris was disappointed to leave Ohio and his horse when his father received orders to report to Torrejon Air Force Base in Spain in 1972.

Navarro's parents promised Chris that they would buy him a new horse once they arrived in Europe. At first reluctant, Chris soon found that he loved the Spanish horse culture. Even better, the air force had a military exhibition rodeo program, and Chris was determined to try it out. His parents were supportive of his riding in the bareback horse competitions but refused to let him ride bulls at first. However, by the time he was seventeen years old, Chris had not only begun riding bulls but had also won the All-Around title of the military rodeo organization. He loved the lifestyle and was determined to keep going.

The love for rodeo brought Navarro back to the United States, and the excellent Animal Science and Rodeo Sports program at Casper College brought him to Wyoming. He had never seen the state before, but he enjoyed its wide-open spaces and abundant wildlife. Throughout his college career, Chris competed as a rodeo cowboy every chance he got. The competition, however, was fierce, with animals that were significantly more powerful than those he had grown used to, and his cowboy rivals had ridden their entire lives. Championships and fame were not in the cards, so he found another way to make a living.

After college, Chris started working in the Wyoming oil fields, beginning with the AMF Turboscope Company. By 1979, he had become a field superintendent and expected that he would work for oil companies for the rest of his life.

By chance, a friend wanted to buy a property he was responsible for while he and Chris were on a hunting trip. The property turned out to be the house of renowned sculptor Harry Jackson, and Chris was mesmerized by what he saw. Jackson's bronze of the legendary horse Steamboat impressed him the most. Even in metal, Chris could sense the horse's power and movement. Having loved and studied art as a child, Chris realized that he could capture the grace and strength of the horse through sculpture himself. With that epiphany, Chris decided to become a sculptor himself.

Navarro began his lifelong pursuit as an artist by purchasing supplies from a local art store and checking out as many books on the great master sculptors as he could find at the Casper Library. Chris believes that he has learned his trade from the greatest of sculptors, and his success is undeniable, even though he had no formal training in art. From his humble start in 1979, Chris became a professional sculptor in 1986. He has won many national awards for his works, which are displayed throughout the United States in numerous art shows, galleries, private collections and public venues and range in size from intimate miniatures to sublime monuments. His three-decade love affair with sculpture and lifelong passion for animals has taken him far.

Chris Navarro with
his *Bolt from the Blue*
sculpture. *Starley
Talbott photograph.*

"I try to become each piece of sculpture. If I'm sculpting a horse, I imagine how he feels as he flies across the ground. I want to capture the power of a buffalo herd surging across the prairie by immersing myself into that buffalo's world. I try to title my pieces to reflect the motion it conveys. As I work on a sculpture, it becomes part of me. I need to sculpt. I feel the clay in my hands and watch it come alive in three dimensions. I don't think life can really be described. It can only be experienced. For me, sculpting captures those experiences," Navarro explained.

"My work has always been intertwined with my life. They say a man needs three things in life for real happiness: someone to love, work that is satisfying and something to hope for. I'm fortunate to have all these things. Family, horses, rodeo and art have been my driving passions, and I hope others can see that through my work," Chris concluded.

ROBIN LAWS, SCULPTOR

From the time she entered first grade in the little two-room schoolhouse at Woodrow, Colorado, Robin Laws knew that she wanted to be an artist. She attended the small rural school fifteen miles south of Brush, Colorado, in first and second grade.

"I had this wonderful first-grade teacher who taught us how to make a mold, fill it with plaster and later paint the marvelous little statues that we created," Robin said. The school had two rooms and a hallway containing a stand with a bucket of water and a dipper to get a drink. There were also separate outhouses for boys and girls. "We didn't have modern accommodations at the school, but we had art, much to my delight," Robin added.

Following her two years in Woodrow, Robin attended school in Brush, Colorado, graduating from high school there. In Brush, another teacher inspired Robin's dreams of becoming an artist. She learned how to do silversmith art and copper enameling and etching. She also took painting and drawing, and she learned the basics of design. However, other teachers did not think it was possible to earn a living with art and told Robin that she should study math and bookkeeping, which Robin didn't find interesting. Soon after high school, she married but later divorced her first husband.

Twenty years later, Robin was living in Fort Morgan, Colorado, and married Myron Laws. She worked for an oil company and was laid off from her job in 1984. Myron suggested that Robin should attend an art show in Denver. She reluctantly agreed, enjoyed the show and met several sculptors from Loveland, Colorado, who encouraged her to visit the Lundeen Studio and a Foundry in Loveland. Laws said that many people helped her along the way, and she met some fabulous folks. In a few years, her art became known in both the United States and several foreign countries. She began traveling to several areas of the world, where her sculptures were purchased and installed. One of her most memorable trips was a cruise, in the 1990s, on the Volga River from St. Petersburg to Moscow, where she was booked to present a class on sculpture. During the twenty-four hours when the cruise ship crossed Lake Onega, Robin helped entertain passengers by talking about the process of creating a sculpture, and she showed the audience her sculpture of a donkey.

Animals are the favorite topic for many of Robin Laws hundreds of sculptures. Robin and Myron moved to a small acreage east of Cheyenne in 2000. Soon their farm was occupied by horses, donkeys, goats, chickens, ducks, dogs and cats. Many of Robin's sculptures are modeled from her beloved pets.

Robin Laws with her statue of a donkey. *Starley Talbott photograph.*

Laws worked with Harvey Deselms at his art gallery in Cheyenne before she moved to Wyoming. When Harvey discussed the Capitol Avenue Bronze Project with Robin, she was excited to provide the first new statue along Capitol Avenue near St. Mary's Cathedral. The sculpture, *In Good Hands*, was chosen by Nathaniel Trelease to honor his mother. The statue features an angel watching over several animals that were created from memories of some of Robin's favorite pets, including the donkey Jennifer, the dog Puff, the bunny Buck and the cat Della. "Those animals, who had died, needed an angel to watch over them so they would be in Good Hands," Robin said. Her statues of *Kittens and Cream*, *The Guardian* and others along 17th Avenue in Cheyenne stand as a testimony to Robin's devotion to animals.

Robin has had numerous works exhibited in many places, including the Old West Museum and Deselms Fine Art Gallery in Cheyenne; Expressions Gallery in Sheridan, Wyoming; and Manitou Gallery in Santa Fe, New Mexico. Following the death of her husband, Myron Laws, Robin stays busy on the farm near Cheyenne. She has help from her two daughters and three granddaughters. She continues to sculpt, inspired by her beloved animals, and she says, "I can't think of a better way to spend a lifetime."

TANNER LOREN, SCULPTOR

One could say that Tanner Loren is a late bloomer. Following graduation from Cody High School, the Wyoming native was not sure what path he wanted to take for his future. He loved studying history, but he did not believe that he wanted to be a teacher. Perhaps fate intervened when he began working at Caleco Foundry in Cody in 2004.

For nearly twenty years, Loren developed artistic skills while honing the crafts of a welder and metal chaser. The foundry produced sculptures for world-class artists. Tanner worked hand in hand with artists who also mentored him to become an artist in his own right. He explained the craft of turning a lump of clay into a fine bronze statue, involving a process of casting the sculpture in bronze. Tanner said that some sculptures are cast in pieces. It was his job to weld the pieces together and then, as a "metal chaser," to smooth the welded parts into a fine texture for the finished statue.

While working at the foundry, Tanner developed a passion for sculpting and began creating his own art. He developed his own style and learned about the details of life that would help him to become a working artist himself. This experience proved valuable as he moved from casting the work of other artists to creating his own sculptures.

The artistic life of Tanner Loren burst into full bloom in 2020 when the Cody Heritage Museum added his life-size bronze statue *Work to Be Done* to its heritage garden. The statue features a pioneer man and woman looking out over the vast landscape, with shovel and hoe in hand, prepared for the work to be done to build a community.

Loren had spent his youth working on a family-owned cattle ranch. He developed a keen sense of appreciation for the western way of life through his experiences at the ranch. Drawing on his love of history, Tanner strives to capture the essence of his work by bringing to life western, wildlife and historical sculptures, including Native Americans, mountain men, cowboys and cavalry soldiers. Adding to his competency, Tanner does most of the foundry work for his statues, from the wax creation to pouring bronze, welding and metal chasing the final product.

Loren has some of his work displayed at the Power River Gallery in Cheyenne, and he has participated in the Western Spirit Art Show at the Old West Museum. He is well represented in the Capitol Avenue Bronze Project. Three of these statues capturing Wyoming history include for John Colter, *Mountain Man*; Chief Yellow Calf, *Arapahoe Chief*; and a *Sheep Wagon*.

Tanner Loren holds his sculpture of *John Colter*, along with the plaque for the Colter statue. *Starley Talbott photograph.*

John Colter was a member of the Lewis and Clark Expedition from 1804 to 1806. He is also remembered for explorations he made during the winter of 1807 to 1808, when he became the first known person of European descent to enter the region that later became Yellowstone National Park and to see the Teton Mountain Range. Colter spent much time alone in the wilderness and is considered to be the first known mountain man, traversing much of Wyoming and the West.

Chief Yellow Calf, who lived from 1861 to 1938, is considered one of the Northern Arapaho tribe's most important and respected leaders in its history and was the last chief of the tribe in Wyoming. Descendants of the chief's family still reside on Wyoming's Wind River Reservation. Loren was fortunate to meet with members of the family, including Matt Wallowing Bull, who invited him to participate in a Sweat Lodge Ceremony featuring the performance of traditional songs. "That was an experience I will forever treasure," said Tanner.

The *Sheep Wagon* sculpture is one quarter of the size of a real sheep wagon, representing the state's long association with sheep ranching.

In preparation for creating a sculpture, Loren conducted enormous research and created a back story for the character to be represented. "I try to breathe life into the statue I am creating," Tanner said. He has learned to sew and makes costumes representing the character he is creating. He attends Mountain Man Rendezvous dressed as a mountain man. A future goal is to visit all the forts in Wyoming.

In addition to traveling in 2023, Loren Tanner added to his lifetime experience when he married the love of his life, Stephanie, on April 22, 2023. He also welcomed three sons, Kenneth, Ben and Josh into his life.

"I love history—that is what helped me to eventually become an artist," Tanner concluded.

JOEY BAINER, SCULPTOR

A recipe for success includes a passion for art, along with a dose of hard work, achieved by Colorado sculpture artist Joey Bainer.

Bainer graduated from Thompson Valley High School in Loveland, Colorado, in 2007. He wasn't interested in attending college, and he wanted to become a sculptor. Fortunately for Joey, he became employed by the Lundeen Studios in Loveland. The Lundeen family has assisted many young artists to learn the sculpture process.

Joey spent six years learning about the process of creating a bronze sculpture. He asked many questions along the way, while following the steps for producing a sculpture used by Lundeen Studios. The process begins by creating a clay sculpture followed by several additional steps, including adding a thin rubber layer to the clay, pouring a wax replica and sending the mold to the foundry for casting. When the sculpture is returned from the foundry, it is usually in many different pieces. The original artist often completes the sculpture and spends hours welding the pieces back together, "metal chasing" or smoothing the welded seams and then polishing and adding a patina to complete the bronze sculpture.

Bainer left the Lundeen Studios in 2013 to work at a mannequin factory in Broomfield, Colorado, for two years. He then returned to Lundeen, where he was invited to join a team creating a prominent Stations of the Cross sculpture for the Cloisters on the Platte Commission. The Cloisters is a 932-acre retreat center near Omaha, Nebraska, featuring a 2,500-foot-long walking tour featuring the fourteen sculptures representing the Stations of the Cross. Bainer was the sculptor for six of the stations. With the earnings from that endeavor, Joey was able to establish his own studio in Loveland.

In addition to his own work, Bainer also continues to contribute to additional works with Lundeen Studios, including these sculptures: *Crew of Apollo XIII* for the Johnson Space Center in Houston; *The Eagle Has Landed: Crew of Apollo XI* for the Kennedy Space Center in Florida; and *Sally Ride* for the Cradle of Aviation Museum in Garden City, Long Island, New York.

Along with the creative aspects of producing a sculpture, Bainer is devoted to the idea that "an artist is responsible for attempting to shine a light on stories and ideas that people don't generally know about."

Bainer's work for the Capitol Avenue Bronze Project includes *Comparing Time*, a statue that tells about the implementation of using standard time by the railroads to assist in creating safe schedules for trains. He also created the sculpture *Pump Jack* to honor the role the oil industry has played in Wyoming.

Joey Bainer touches up the clay mold for the *Princess Blue Water* sculpture. *Starley Talbott photograph.*

The bronze sculpture project in Cheyenne has expanded beyond Capitol Avenue to the installation of sculptures along many other streets in the city. Bainer is working on additional sculptures to add to the history of the area, including a bronze of Sioux Native Princess Blue Water and a statue of the outlaw Tom Horn.

"Art can transcend time so that people look at life in different ways and perhaps change perspectives"—such is the belief that Joey Bainer brings to the sculptures he creates for public display.

RICH HAINES, SCULPTOR

Wyoming sculptor Rich Haines has an appreciation and fondness for western and wildlife art. Rich was born and raised in Cheyenne, where he developed an appreciation for the art of sculpture through a class at his high school.

Specializing in wildlife and themes of the West, Rich's bronze sculptures can be found in both private and public collections across the region. Perhaps his most well-known sculpture is the ram in front of Moby Arena on the campus of Colorado State University in Fort Collins.

Haines has two sculptures among the Capitol Avenue bronze statues: *My Red Tricycle* and *Norma's Calf*. The little boy on the tricycle is reminiscent of a quiet and carefree time. The baby calf pays a tribute to Wyoming's agriculture.

When Haines was in high school and taking a sculpture class, he worked for Harvey Deselms in Deselms Fine Art Gallery. Rich was invited to visit the ranch of Harvey's parents, Kenneth and Norma, in Albin, Wyoming. During the visit, Haines captured a photograph of a baby calf that was Norma Deselms's favorite calf because it had to be fed with a bucket when the mother cow was unable to provide for the tiny calf.

The photograph of the baby calf later became the inspiration for Haines to create the sculpture *Norma's Calf*, which resides on the Northeast Corner of Capitol Avenue and 17th Street. The statue was donated by the Deselms family as an appropriate way to honor Kenneth and Norma Deselms.

Each piece of art that Haines creates is intended to be a true representation of the subject's character rather than a stylized or symbolic image. Haines believes that an artist can only successfully create that of which they have knowledge, and this is the reason why he receives satisfaction from his subject matter.

CHRISTINE KNAPP, SCULPTOR

Telling a story is important to artist Christine Knapp. As both a painter and a sculptor, Knapp believes that any medium conveyed by the artist should tell the viewer a story.

Although Knapp arrived at becoming a sculpture artist after years of producing artistic paintings and spending more than forty years as a nurse, she found her passion when she completed her first sculpture of an eagle in 1990.

Knapp grew up in Dayton, Ohio, the eldest of five children in her family. Although her parents allowed her to draw and paint, they wanted her to pursue a career that would provide a more predictable income than becoming an artist. So, Knapp opted to become a nurse and graduated from nursing school in 1971. She met her future husband, Bill Knapp, during her first hospital assignment where he served as an orderly. They married and became the parents of two boys.

Life as a nurse and mother consumed much of her time, but Knapp still painted and attended artistic workshops when possible. As a lover of animals, especially horses, Christine attended a workshop in Montana on painting and sculpture, where she also planned to enjoy the opportunity of horseback riding. During the workshop she became so engrossed in learning to make a sculpture that she never got around to riding a horse.

Knapp continued to provide a major source of income for her family as a nurse while her husband attended law school and eventually began his own business as a lawyer. Their sons grew up and graduated from The Ohio State University. Along the way, Christine sold a few paintings and saved her earnings to pursue sculpting by attending additional workshops. She also

Christine Knapp with her statue of a mountain lion and cubs in front of the Nagle Warren Mansion on 17th Street in Cheyenne. *Starley Talbott photograph.*

traveled to South America, Canada, Europe and Africa to gain firsthand knowledge of the animals she enjoyed sculpting.

In 1990, Knapp applied to enter her work in the Loveland Sculpture Show in Colorado and was accepted. To her amazement, several of her animal sculptures sold at the show, and she has continued to exhibit there for several years. Knapp also exhibited at other art shows throughout the United States and has won numerous awards, including Best of Show at the Sioux Falls Sculpture Walk in South Dakota in 2022.

Encouraged by her awards and the sale of her sculptures, Knapp realized that it might be possible to earn a living with her art. After tiring of making the long drive to Colorado from Ohio several times, Christine and Bill decided to move to Lyons, Colorado, in 2008. However, Christine didn't give up her nursing career, even though she did not enjoy it. She worked as a nurse in the cardiac unit of the Longmont, Colorado hospital for several years before resigning.

Knapp is a self-taught artist and workshop-trained artist. She also began teaching workshops in painting along with a co-artist who taught sculpture during summer sessions lasting a few weeks. Eventually, she also taught sculpting workshops. "When you teach, you learn as much as your students do. I also encourage my students to draw because I believe drawing is important to creating a painting or a sculpture. Drawing your subject over and over again from different angles helps with perspective," Christine says.

Beginning in 2013, Knapp taught summer art classes at the Western Art Academy of Schreiner University in Kerrville, Texas, for six years. She had also previously taught a class in Dubois, Wyoming, where she was encouraged by one of her students to contact Harvey Deselms in Cheyenne, who owned an art gallery there.

A conversation with Deselms led to Christine's participation in the Capitol Avenue Bronze Project being curated by Deselms. She provided the sculpture *My Little Deer* on the northeast corner of Capitol Avenue and 18th Street of a mule deer similar to her statue of a white-tailed deer that is on display in Hawaii.

Knapp had previously shipped three bronze sculptures to Kauai, Hawaii, for inclusion in the Na Aina Kai Botanical Gardens. Those statues of a moose, a caribou and a white-tail deer are among her favorite sculptures, and she was able to see them there on a recent trip to Hawaii.

Sculpture has now become the focus of Christine Knapp's artistic story. "It took me a while to realize art has value and meaning, while adding to the story by providing a personal interpretation to the viewer," she concluded.

MARTHA PETTIGREW, SCULPTOR

A love of all animals, especially horses, led Martha Pettigrew to begin her sculpture career in 1992. After raising horses for many years, Martha created her first sculpture of a horse, and she never looked back.

Pettigrew grew up in Lincoln, Nebraska, and graduated from the University of Nebraska–Lincoln in 1972 with a Bachelor of Fine Arts degree. She specialized in painting and printmaking and took a few classes in sculpture. She spent six years as a scientific illustrator for the Nebraska State Museum in Lincoln. In 1978, she married Delmar Pettigrew, and they raised horses among other pursuits.

Eventually, both Martha and "Del" became sculpture artists. Following the demise of one of their business ventures, Martha decided to become a bronze sculpture artist. She did not take any sculpture classes, but she became involved with the Art Castings Foundry in Loveland, Colorado, where her artistic molds were cast at its foundry.

Martha Pettigrew with her *Beaver Pond* statue. *Starley Talbott photograph.*

Along with sculpturing horses, Martha also enjoys sculpting other animals and Native American figures. She was originally known as a Southwest artist, but she is now known for many types of art. She is also a painter, and she currently displays her paintings and sculptures at five galleries: Legacy Manitou Gallery in Santa Fe, New Mexico; Sanders Gallery in Tucson, Arizona; Tubac Gallery in Arizona; Big Horn Gallery in Cody, Wyoming; and Deselms Fine Art Gallery in Cheyenne, Wyoming.

One of Martha's figurative sculptures, *Gossip*, is on permanent display at the Grounds for Sculpture Museum, Sculpture Garden and Arboretum in Hamilton, New Jersey. The sculpture park opened in 1992 on the former New Jersey State Fairgrounds and exhibits three hundred sculptures on forty-two landscaped acres.

Del Pettigrew assisted Martha when she began her career in sculpture. Eventually, he decided to become a sculpture artist too, and he spent twenty years sculpting animals. Martha said that Del had no formal training as an artist, but he knew animals, as he had raised racehorses for thirty years.

Del and Martha spent ten weeks every winter, for twenty-six years, exhibiting their work at the Celebration of Fine Art show in Scottsdale, Arizona. The couple set up their exhibit in one of the large tents, where they interacted with other artists and the public. "It was a lot of work, but we enjoyed meeting people there, and we were the top sellers at the show for ten years," Martha said.

The Pettigrews lived in Lincoln, Nebraska, when they began sculpting. They traveled often to Loveland, Colorado, to take their sculpted molds to the foundry. On one trip from Loveland back to Lincoln, Del remarked, as they drove through Kearney, Nebraska, "We would be home by now if we lived in Kearney." So, they packed up and moved to Kearney, where Martha continues to live and work. Del Pettigrew died in 2017 and "left a legacy in art of the animals he created," Martha said.

Martha has one sculpture, *Dakota Wind*, on Capitol Avenue. The sculpture is a scale model of a larger statue on display in Sioux Falls, South Dakota. *Dakota Wind* depicts a Native woman wrapped in a buffalo robe to protect her against the wind and cold—typical weather conditions on the western prairies. Del also has a sculpture on Capitol Avenue titled *Earning His Oats*. The statue depicts a draft horse in harness pulling a load up an incline, a symbol of persistence and tenacity when performing any type of work.

Since the beginning of Martha Pettigrew's sculpture career, she has poured her heart and soul into her work, and she has been able to make a living from the products she has created.

DON JONES, STONEMASON/BRICKLAYER

Many different artists have applied their talents to the bronze statues that grace Capitol Avenue. Each bronze is enhanced by a stone pedestal that holds the statue. Most of the pedestals were created by the artistry of Don Jones.

Jones is a fifth-generation bricklayer. He was born in Laramie, Wyoming, and began working in the family business as a hod carrier at the age of twelve. Don advanced to become an apprentice bricklayer when he was twenty years old and a journeyman at the age of twenty-three.

While working for the Jones family business in Laramie, Don earned his nickname. He lived for a time in a mobile home near the company's storage area to serve as a guard because of vandalism and theft in the area. When his uncle returned from a vacation, he greeted his nephew with these words: "There is Donnie Dog, the Brickyard Watchdog." The name stuck, and most everyone who knows Don Jones fondly calls him "The Dog."

Jones moved to Cheyenne in 1986, the same year he and his wife, Karen, were married. He worked at various occupations, including a laborer, cement finisher and carpenter. In 1989, he was hired by a contractor to help build

Don Jones, master stonemason, also known as "Don the Dog," relaxing in his workshop. *Starley Talbott photograph.*

Don Jones cutting a piece of stone for the pedestal of a sculpture. *Starley Talbott photograph.*

the Wyoming National Guard's new fire department and cafeteria at the Cheyenne airport.

A new opportunity arrived for Jones in 1990 when he was hired by Jim Johnson of HFJ Masonry of Cheyenne, where he still works today. Within a few months, Don became the masonry foreman, and two years later, he was the general superintendent for HFJ Masonry. The company performed many jobs throughout Wyoming and beyond. Jones is most proud of working on an addition to the Wyoming Supreme Court building in Cheyenne.

Don is semi-retired at present but was requested to build the stone pedestals for the bronze statue project in Cheyenne. He was told that there would be twenty-seven statues, but as of 2023, he had built more than sixty stone pedestals—and more are expected.

Jones said, "I can't retire until all the pedestals are finished. I still enjoy working as a bricklayer and stonemason."

PART III

THE BRONZE
SCULPTURES

FRANCIS E. WARREN

Location: Capitol Avenue and 23rd Street, in front of the Hathaway Building
Artist: Guadalupe Barajas
Donors: Gordon and Beverly Black

No one would have probably thought much of the young man who stepped off the train in Cheyenne in May 1868. It was a bustling boomtown filled with railroaders, miners, transients and all manner of people looking to carve their livelihoods out of the chilly, windswept plains at the foot of the Rockies.

From his perspective, the man saw a town of makeshift buildings, designed to be moved from one place to another, tents and cobbled-together log structures. One might wonder what drew this man to this point on the Transcontinental Railroad, which by this time had just crossed through Sherman Pass into the valley beyond where Laramie City was taking shape. It was a wild and lawless place, but Francis Emory Warren had been pulled by the lure of the West, where he was to find his destiny.

Warren was twenty-three years old when he reached Cheyenne. A native of Massachusetts, he was a seasoned veteran of the Civil War, as he joined the Union army in September 1862 as a private in Company C of the 49th Massachusetts Infantry. On May 27, 1863, Warren, along with the rest of the men, stormed a Confederate artillery battery at Port Hudson, Mississippi, defended by 6,800 men. The poorly coordinated attack failed, and Warren was nearly killed from a serious scalp wound, from which he recovered.

As the weather warmed, the people of Cheyenne wondered if their hell-on-wheels town would survive, and many thought it a good idea to abandon the town and move west following the advancing railroad. Warren waved off such pessimistic talk since he was an experienced farm foreman with skills in carpentry and blacksmithing. Such talent was needed in the new town, and work was plentiful.

In 1871, Asa Converse, another Massachusetts transplant who took a chance on Cheyenne, hired Warren to work in his new dry goods store. The two men became friends and then partners. Warren proved to be a deft businessman, and the company thrived. That same year, he married Helen M. Smith, also of Massachusetts.

Within the year of establishing his prosperity and matrimonial bliss, Warren discovered that he also had a knack for local politics when he won a Republican seat on the Wyoming territorial legislature in the election of 1872. At the age of thirty, he maneuvered himself to become the president of the upper house of the legislature and secured a place on the Cheyenne City Council in 1873, a position he would hold for the next decade. He became the Wyoming territorial treasurer in 1876, serving for several years.

Warren broadened his business interests wherever he could, frequently striving to make Cheyenne the best community it could be and profiting as a result. In 1882, he partnered with several other businessmen in establishing the Cheyenne Opera House, one of the finest in the nation, and secured a controlling interest in the tiny Cheyenne and Northern Railway. In 1883, he became president of the Brush-Swan Electric Company and was responsible for installing the first electric street lighting in Cheyenne, being one of the very earliest cities in the United States to do so.

The vast amount of money that allowed Warren to thrive in Cheyenne was the result of the massive cattle industry that had sprung up in Wyoming. For more than a decade, raising beef had been the source of more wealth for Cheyenne and Wyoming than any other. Warren had also been successful in the business, and in 1883, he founded the giant Warren Livestock Company, which gradually grew to encompass 150,000 acres of land where he raised sheep as well as cattle.

Warren became Cheyenne's mayor for a brief time in January 1885. Near the same time that Warren ascended to guide the city, William Hale, the territorial governor, died of a long-term illness. President Chester A. Arthur appointed Warren to be Wyoming's new territorial governor.

Warren soon faced a major challenge. On September 2, 1885, the miners of Rock Springs, angered by brutal Union Pacific Coal Company policies and suspicion of unfair treatment, rioted and killed twenty-eight Chinese workers before driving the rest out of town. Alerted to the shocking news, Warren headed to Rock Springs the next morning by rail. Seeing that the town was still being rocked by violence, Warren proceeded to Evanston, where he called on the president for military aid. Three companies from Utah and Fort D.A. Russell were dispatched to quell the uprising. The Union Pacific praised Warren's actions to the president in a letter. Other men in Washington took note of Warren's quick actions as well and looked on him favorably. These prevailing attitudes toward him allowed Warren to remain in office for twenty months into Grover Cleveland's Democratic administration before he was asked to resign.

When the Republican-dominated Wyoming territorial legislature convened in January 1886, Francis E. Warren proposed that funds be expended for new health services for Wyoming's citizens. The first proposal was for the creation of a school for the "deaf and dumb" in Cheyenne, one of the first major efforts to support people with disabilities in the territory. While that effort failed to gain traction, his second proposal, this time for an insane asylum, bore fruit. At his prodding, the Wyoming territorial legislature founded the first dedicated mental health facility in Wyoming at Evanston. Through a series of well-supported proposals, the legislature approved the construction of a new territorial capitol building in Cheyenne and the University of Wyoming in Laramie. Additionally, new legislation was put forward to put new safety regulations in the territory's coal mines and to ban children under a certain age and women from working in the mines. The legislature also divided the territory into water districts and established rules for creating irrigation projects. Significantly, the legislature also took advantage of new federal laws allowing for the taxation of railroads and homesteaders, thereby creating a source of stable funding for the territory.

When Republican Benjamin Harrison assumed the presidency, he again invited Warren to be Wyoming's governor. Warren agreed and returned to the office in 1888. Through his efforts, aided by allies such as Joseph M. Carey, Warren launched the effort to secure Wyoming statehood. Without Congressional approval, Warren convened an election to create a constitutional convention in July 1889. The delegates convened in September and assembled the state's constitution, which was approved by the Wyoming public on November 5. Members of Congress decried the fact that they had not granted Warren permission to call a constitutional convention; still

Francis E. Warren memorial. *Starley Talbott photograph.*

others argued that Wyoming did not have enough population and, worse, allowed women to vote. Undeterred, Joseph M. Carey presented the case for Wyoming statehood on the House floor in March 1890. Buoyed by strong Republican support in both chambers of Congress, the bill to grant statehood passed. Wyoming became the forty-fourth state of the Union on July 10, 1890. Warren won the election to become the State of Wyoming's first governor. He surrendered the governorship after being in office two months when he was selected to return to the U.S. Senate.

When Warren, now forty-six, entered the halls of the Senate, he was the junior senator to Joseph M. Carey. The two men had previously been cordial, but the politics of Washington changed the game. The relationship became difficult, and the only legislation that they agreed on was the Carey Act, which would open vast portions of the American West to irrigation and settlement. They took opposing positions on the free-silver issue, where Carey strongly opposed the coining of silver by the U.S. mint, while Warren deferred to the will of Wyoming public, which was in favor. Another serious point in which the men differed was on how to manage the eruption of the Johnson County War back in Wyoming in 1892. Both men were members of the Wyoming Stock Growers Association and were fully in support of the invasion. When it failed, Carey responded by burning papers that may have demonstrated his involvement. Warren professed that he was in the dark about the invaders' actions until it became national news. Even so, he still supported their actions as being those of just men seeking to protect their property.

Warren returned to Wyoming after losing his Senate seat. Through the efforts of allies across Wyoming, including those of his friend Willis Van Devanter, Carey lost his position as Wyoming's senator, and Warren took his place in the elections of 1895.

Wyoming had a tremendously powerful advocate in Warren, and he advanced benefits for Wyoming's people at every opportunity. He hired

Leona Wells as the first woman to be a Senate staff member. She served as his personal secretary for thirty years, and she was eventually joined by two hundred other women Senate staffers before she retired.

The ascent of Warren's star seemed unstoppable, but he was struck by personal tragedy twice. In 1902, Helen died after a lengthy illness. In 1911, he married Clara LeBaron Morgon, thirty-two years younger than Warren. Tragedy struck again in 1915 when one of his two daughters, Frances, and three of her children died in a tragic fire at the Presidio in California. Warren grieved the loss alongside his son-in-law, General John J. "Blackjack" Pershing, whom he had helped elevate to his rank of brigadier general. When the United States joined World War I in 1917, Pershing was placed in command of the American Expeditionary Forces. For his part, Warren was the ranking minority member of the powerful Senate Appropriations Committee, where he helped fund and equip American forces that Pershing led.

After the war, Warren continued to advocate for Wyoming and supported both the Nineteenth Amendment, which gave all American women the right to vote, and the Twentieth Amendment, banning the manufacture and sale of alcohol within the United States. A staunch supporter of tariffs, Warren continuously fought to protect Wyoming agriculture from foreign competition, which was particularly helpful as the state struggled economically after the Great War.

On November 24, 1929, Warren died from pneumonia. He was hailed as the "Dean of the Senate" because he had served longer than any senator in history up to that time. He had been awarded the Congressional Medal of Honor for his military service. His funeral was held in the Senate chambers, and he was buried at Cheyenne's Lakeview Cemetery. In tribute to his long and exemplary service to Wyoming and the nation, President Herbert Hoover renamed Fort D.A. Russell to Fort Francis E. Warren in 1930.

The record and actions of Francis E. Warren know no parallel in the history of Wyoming. No one could have known who the young man was who stepped off the train in Cheyenne in 1868—or who he would become. Warren could aptly be called one of the founding fathers of Wyoming.

Among the donors of the Warren sculpture is Beverly Black, the great-granddaughter of Benjamin Franklin Ketcham. Her great-grandfather Benjamin Ketcham arrived in Cheyenne at about the same time that Francis Warren arrived in the city. Ketcham came to work briefly for the railroad, and then he established a ranch on the west side of Cheyenne.

Beverly Black provided a few anecdotes about the connection between Ketcham and Warren. Benjamin Ketcham operated the first dairy in Cheyenne, and he delivered milk and meat to residents. Following the erection of the state capitol building, Ketcham became involved in politics and delivered a speech on the steps of the capitol. Governor Warren objected to the topic of the speech, and the two men engaged in a fistfight on the capitol steps. Beverly Black is not certain who won the fight, but the two men knew each other.

Ketcham owned land in several locations near Cheyenne, including the future Wyoming Angus Ranch on Happy Jack Road. He eventually established a ranch in Colorado, just two miles from the Wyoming border. Ketcham's dairy cows were lost in a blizzard in the late 1800s and ended up finding shelter and water southeast of Cheyenne across the state line in Colorado. Ketcham noticed that the location was sheltered and had several water springs, and he decided to file a claim on that land when it became available. Several generations have resided on the ranch he established there, Eagle Rock Ranch, and it is today the home of Beverly Black and her husband, Gordon. They decided to donate the sculpture of Francis E. Warren because of his connection to Beverly's great-grandfather.

The plaque reads, "Senator Francis E. Warren by Guadalupe Barajas. Donated to the city of Cheyenne by the Wyoming Angus Ranch and the descendants of Benjamin Franklin Ketcham 2022."

NELLIE TAYLOE ROSS

Location: Capitol Avenue and 23rd Street, in front of the Hathaway Building
Artist: Joel Turner
Donors: Dixie and Tom Roberts

Nellie Tayloe Ross is honored with two bronze statues in Cheyenne, Wyoming, where she served as the first woman governor in Wyoming and the nation. Her statue on Capitol Avenue stands near the Wyoming Capitol, where she was sworn in as governor on January 5, 1925. Nellie's second statue stands in front of the historic Governor's Mansion, where she lived as first lady of Wyoming and as governor of Wyoming.

Nellie Tayloe was born November 29, 1876, in Missouri. Nellie became a schoolteacher after receiving her education. In 1902, she married William Ross, and the couple moved to Cheyenne. William entered the practice of law and was elected as Wyoming's governor in 1922. William died suddenly on October 2, 1924, due to complications from appendicitis.

Nellie Tayloe Ross memorial. *Starley Talbott photograph.*

Nellie was nominated as the Democratic candidate for the unexpired term of William Ross. She won the election and became the first female governor in the United States. Nellie was dressed all in black for the inauguration ceremony and delivered a brief statement, including these words: "My election calls forth in this solemn hour my deepest gratitude and challenges me to rise to the opportunities for service thus made possible, and to dedicate to the task before me every faculty of mind and body with which I may be endowed."

As governor, Nellie Ross was a champion of women's rights and stressed the need for tax relief for farmers. She proposed legislation to require counties, school boards and the state council to prepare budgets and publish them before levying taxes. Her proudest achievement was enacting a law compelling the use of safety devices in coal mines and more thorough mine inspections. At the end of her term in 1926, Nellie was defeated for reelection by Republican Frank Emerson.

Nathaniel Trelease giving the statue of Nellie Tayloe Ross a ride to her place on Capitol Avenue. *Starley Talbott photograph.*

After her defeat, Nellie embarked on a career of writing and speechmaking on the national Chautauqua circuit. Presidential candidate Al Smith appointed her vice-chairman of the Democratic National Committee in 1928, where she served for four years.

Nellie wrote several articles for *Good Housekeeping* magazine in which she reminisced about her term as Wyoming's governor. She expressed her admiration for the people of Wyoming and her love for the state:

> *In every little town and settlement, in the lonely homestead as well as in the large ranch, in the tang of the sagebrush even, and in the brilliance of the Indian Paintbrush, Wyoming's state flower, flaming on the hills, I found delight…often at a turn in the road there would suddenly burst upon my view long stretches of beautiful and fertile valleys. Checkered with fields of*

varied crops, they looked like cross patch quilts, and I was as proud of the productivity as if I had cultivated every patch with my own hand. My chief pleasure, however, was the interesting companionships that always awaited me at the end of the journey.

Following his election for president, Franklin D. Roosevelt appointed Nellie Tayloe Ross to be the first female director of the U.S. Mint in 1933. She ran the mint as an efficient and humane executive for the next twenty years.

Nellie remained in Washington, D.C., following her retirement from the Mint and stated, "I am grateful for all that the wonderful people of Wyoming have done for me." Nellie Tayloe Ross died on December 19, 1977, at the age of 101.

The donors of Nellie's statues are Dixie and Tom Roberts. Dixie and Tom are active in many aspects of giving back to the community. Tom is a retired attorney, and Dixie is the owner and operator of Ameriprise Financial.

In many ways, Dixie Roberts could be compared to Nellie Tayloe Ross. Both women have shown care and compassion for their communities. Robert's long list of participation in giving back to her community lives up to her statement, "You have to pay rent for the space you occupy."

Dixie Sims moved with her family to Cheyenne when she was six months old and has lived in Cheyenne ever since. Dixie graduated from Central High School in 1973, attended Laramie County Community College and the University of Wyoming and earned a master's degree from the University of Colorado–Greeley.

As a child growing up in Cheyenne, Dixie admired the tenacity of her parents and learned the value of working to achieve one's goals. As a sixteen-year-old, Dixie and her siblings were helping on the family's chicken farm east of Cheyenne. "We gathered the eggs, culled them, washed them, sorted and boxed the eggs and delivered them to various locations," she said.

As an adult, many of Dixie's civic achievements began when she graduated from the Leadership Cheyenne program, hosted by the Greater Cheyenne Chamber of Commerce, in 1989. From there she went on to serving as president of the Cheyenne Chamber of Commerce, chair of the Wyoming Healthcare Commission, chair of the Cheyenne Regional Medical Center, chair of Cheyenne LEADS and on several other board positions.

Active in the Cheyenne Kiwanis Club, Dixie served as president and was the chair of the Kiwanis Club sponsorship of the pancake breakfast for the 100th celebration of Cheyenne Frontier Days™. The committee, comprising all women, served 39,111 people in three days, a record that stands to this day.

Four former Wyoming governors. *From left*: Francis E. Warren, Nellie Tayloe Ross, Robert Carey and John Kendrick, circa 1925. *Wyoming State Archives, Department of State Parks and Cultural Resources.*

Dixie was the recipient of the 2022 Community Spirit Award presented by the *Wyoming Tribune Eagle*. The award honors individuals who have volunteered their time and efforts to make Cheyenne a better place to live.

The Robertses are happy to support the Capitol Avenue Bronze Legacy honoring the history of Cheyenne and Wyoming. They have sponsored three statues on Capitol Avenue: *My Red Tricycle*, *Family Ties* and one of Nellie Tayloe Ross, along with additional bronzes in other locations. Dixie is especially proud to honor Nellie Tayloe Ross, whom she believes is "a very special woman that deserves recognition."

The plaque reads, "Nellie Tayloe Ross 1876–1977 by Joel Turner. First elected female governor in the United Sates November 24, 1924. First Woman appointed as Director of the United States Mint 1933–1953. Buried in Lakeview Cemetery at 101 years old. Donated by Dixie and Tom Roberts 2023."

ESTHER HOBART MORRIS

Location: Capitol Avenue and 23ʳᵈ Street, in front of the Supreme Court building
Artist: Joel Turner
Donor: Jim Collins

Esther Hobart Morris is honored in front of Wyoming's Supreme Court building because she served as the first female justice of the peace in Wyoming and the nation. She was appointed as a justice in South Pass City, Wyoming, in 1870 and served in that capacity for eight months.

Morris became a national figure in the women's suffrage movement because of her appointment as justice of the peace. She cast her first vote in an election on September 6, 1870, in South Pass City. Morris was a supporter of women's right to vote, which had been signed into law on December 10, 1869, in Wyoming's territorial legislature.

An invitation to attend the 1871 National Women Suffrage Convention in Washington, D.C., was declined by Morris. She accepted an invitation and attended the American Suffrage Association Convention in San Francisco in 1872.

In 1890, Wyoming became the forty-fourth state admitted to the Union and retained the women's suffrage rights within the state's constitution. Esther Morris presented a forty-four-star silk flag to Governor Francis E. Warren during the statehood celebration on July 23, 1890.

In 1960, upon the request of Wyoming senator Lester Hunt, a statue of Esther Morris was placed in the rotunda of the U.S. Capitol. On December 8, 1963, a replica of the statue was placed in front of the Wyoming Capitol. Senator Hunt recommended Morris for the honor because she had been the first female justice of the peace in the nation and because she played a role in Wyoming's passage of women's suffrage. During the 2019 restoration of the Wyoming Capitol, Esther's statue was moved inside the building.

The bronze sculpture of Esther Hobart Morris was placed on Capitol Avenue in 2022, where her statue looks toward the Wyoming Capitol. Esther had moved to Cheyenne in 1881 to join her son, E.A. Slack, who was the publisher of the *Cheyenne Sun* newspaper. She lived in a cottage on Warren Avenue, where she remained active in Cheyenne and enjoyed her grandchildren. In 1895, Esther attended the National Convention of the Republican Leagues in Cleveland, Ohio, as a delegate from Wyoming. Esther died in 1902 and is buried at Lakeview Cemetery.

Esther Hobart Morris memorial. *Starley Talbott photograph.*

In addition to the bronze statue honoring Esther Morris, a sign has been placed next to her former home on Warren Avenue honoring her service as a judge and an advocate for women's rights.

Donor Jim Collins sponsored the Morris sculpture in honor of his wife, Beverly, who died in 2015. Beverly worked at the Wyoming State Museum in Cheyenne and admired Esther Hobart Morris.

Jim and Beverly Collins moved to Cheyenne in the 1960s, when Jim was a senior field engineer for the Intercontinental Ballistic Missile Program. They had lived in many other areas, and Jim said that they were "Missile Gypsies," following the program in several areas of the United States. Their four children were in junior high school when they reached Cheyenne, and they decided that the city was the best place to call home.

Jim Collins grew up in the village of Massena, New York, and received a technical degree from the State University of New York. He was employed by Rockwell International.

In addition to many activities enjoyed by the Collins family, Jim became interested in the bronze sculpture project when he attended one of the installations of a statue along Capitol Avenue in 2021. He admired the accomplishments of Esther Hobart Morris and felt that her sculpture would be a fitting legacy to his wife of fifty-six years.

As the father of Mayor Patrick Collins of Cheyenne, Jim is proud of his son's involvement in the Capitol Avenue Bronze Project.

The plaque reads, "In Honor of the Wyoming Woman who was the first woman in the United States of America to hold judicial office. A gift of James Collins in loving memory of his wife Beverly Collins 2022."

WILLIS VAN DEVANTER

Location: Capitol Avenue and 23rd Street, in front of the Supreme Court building
Artist: Joel Turner
Donors: Kim and Rob Dickerson and the family of William H. Vines

Willis Van Devanter arrived in Wyoming Territory in 1884. He is one of the lesser-known citizens of the state, and yet he was one of the most significant people to call Wyoming home.

Van Devanter was born on April 17, 1859, in Marion, Indiana. His father, Isaac Van Devanter, was a prominent local lawyer who became the provost marshal of his Congressional district during the Civil War. Willis attended local schools and developed a love of farming while working summers for his grandfather—he intended to become a farmer himself.

Following high school graduation, however, at the urging of his father, Willis enrolled in Cincinnati Law School. One of his classmates was the future president William Howard Taft, who was one year ahead of him. Willis graduated in 1879 and returned home to join his father's law firm, Van Devanter and Lacey. His father's partner, John W. Lacey, was also Willis's brother-in-law, having married one of Willis's sisters. When Isaac retired in 1884, Lacey and his wife moved to Wyoming, where he had recently been appointed the chief justice of the Wyoming territorial court by President Chester A. Arthur. Not to be left behind, Willis decided to follow John Lacey to Wyoming, along with his wife, Dollie, whom he had married in 1881.

When Willis Van Devanter arrived in Cheyenne, it was in its heyday as not only the capital of Wyoming Territory but also a vast cattle enterprise that had brought tremendous wealth and power to the community. Willis joined the firm of a prominent local Republican lawyer, Charles N. Potter. They focused their efforts primarily on land title cases, with the Burlington Northern railroad as their principal client.

Willis, who had always been interested in politics, quickly engaged with the Wyoming Republican Party and became affiliated with Francis E. Warren, who had recently been made Wyoming's territorial governor. In 1886, Warren asked Van Devanter to join J.W. Blake and Isaac P. Caldwell in revising Wyoming's territorial laws. Warren also asked Van Devanter to draft an appropriations bill to fund the construction of a new territorial capitol in Cheyenne and university buildings in Laramie, which were completed a few years later at a combined cost of $150,000.

Van Devanter's legal prowess, his political talent and his ability to make the right connections were soon to take his political and legal career to stellar heights. In 1887, Willis was elected as Cheyenne's city attorney, and in 1888, he was elected to the Wyoming territorial legislature. President Benjamin Harrison appointed him to the Wyoming Territorial Supreme Court in 1899.

Francis E. Warren wanted to secure Wyoming statehood and asked Van Devanter to aid in the endeavor. Van Devanter consulted with members of the Wyoming Constitutional Convention on drafting the future state's new guiding document. When statehood was achieved on July 10, 1890, Willis Van Devanter's role as a territorial justice concluded.

Willis then returned to private practice, this time with his brother-in-law, John Lacey. They represented significant clients, including the Union Pacific Railroad and the Wyoming Stock Growers Association. Van Devanter's association with Wyoming Stock Growers brought him great notoriety a few years later.

In 1892, the Johnson County War erupted between wealthy cattlemen of the Wyoming Stock Growers Association and homesteaders of Buffalo, Wyoming. The association had accused the people of Johnson County of supporting cattle rustling for years and had finally decided to take matters into its own hands. Its attempted takeover of the county through force of arms backfired, and all the "invaders," including twenty-five Texas gunmen, had to be rescued by the U.S. Army. The participants in the invasion were to be placed on trial in Laramie, and the Wyoming Stock Growers Association asked Van Devanter to intervene on behalf of its members. Many believed that Van Devanter had known about the plot in advance and were unhappy that he was now defending the perpetrators. Whether he knew of the plot in advance or not, Van Devanter proved a supremely able defense attorney.

He successfully had the trial moved from Laramie to Cheyenne and then played a principal role in having all charges dismissed against his clients. The Wyoming public, however, was considerably upset by the affair and took its vengeance out on the Republican Party, to which most of the Wyoming Stock Growers Association belonged, by sweeping the party out of the governorship in that year's elections.

By 1894, the heat from the Johnson County War had cooled considerably, and the fortunes of the Republican Party began to rebound under Van Devanter's leadership as party chairman. Francis E. Warren was reelected to the U.S. Senate, where he had served in 1890 after a brief stint as Wyoming's first statehood governor. When Warren returned to Washington, he relied on Van Devanter to keep him informed of political developments in Wyoming. Van Devanter became a close confidant and personal adviser to Warren, something he would continue to be for the rest of Warren's life.

In 1895, Willis Van Devanter made his first appearance in front of the Supreme Court of the United States, this time representing the State of Wyoming in the case *Ward v. Race Horse*. In July 1895, a group of Bannock Indian families from the Fort Hall Reservation in Idaho hunted elk in the Jackson Hole area while en route to visit relatives in the Wind River Reservation in Wyoming. By treaty, Bannocks were allowed to hunt on any unoccupied land off the reservations and had done so since 1868. However, settlers in the area had become angry at what they considered depredations by the Bannocks. In one altercation, shots were fired, a Bannock was killed, another was wounded and one of their children went missing.

Shortly after the Bannock incident, the Wyoming legislature enacted a law against off-reservation hunting, prompting a legal issue on what law had superiority—a federal treaty or a state law. In cooperation with the Federal Indian Bureau, the State of Wyoming placed the case before the federal courts. Race Horse, a Bannock chief, agreed to plead his people's point of view. Van Devanter defended Wyoming's position, stating that Wyoming's statehood abrogated the federal treaty within its own boundaries. Federal judge Riner disagreed and ruled in favor of Race Horse. Wyoming appealed to the Supreme Court with Van Devanter, who had just received credentials, to argue in front of the Supreme Court, defending the state again. The Supreme Court sided with Wyoming, 7–1.

In 1897, President McKinley named Van Devanter as assistant attorney general assigned to the Department of the Interior, where he indirectly oversaw the nation's public lands. Willis and Dollie Van Devanter moved

Willis Van Devanter memorial. *Starley Talbott photograph.*

to St. Paul, Minnesota, in 1903, following Van Devanter's appointment to the U.S. Court of Appeals for the Eighth Circuit by President Theodore Roosevelt.

President William Howard Taft appointed Van Devanter to the U.S. Supreme Court in 1910. Taft was leery of Van Devanter's qualifications at first. Van Devanter had offered few opinions in comparison to his fellow judges within the Eighth Circuit, and rumors abounded that Van Devanter didn't work hard enough or took too much time to offer his opinions. Willis was appalled by the rumors and made an eloquent appeal to have his name removed from consideration. Taft was impressed by the appeal and appointed Van Devanter to the court.

During the next several years of his tenure on the Supreme Court, Van Devanter's penchant for writing few opinions continued, and his opinions that were published also tended to be the longest. Van Devanter received criticism from numerous citizens. However, legal scholars have commented that Van Devanter's opinions were very clear and left no room to mistake his intentions. His opinions also served as guidelines for the future, with many practicing on the bar relying on his statements as reliable and thoroughly considered. Van Devanter's fellow justices held him in high regard.

William Howard Taft, the former president, became chief justice of the Supreme Court in 1921. He had his initial misgivings about Van Devanter but quickly came to rely on Van Devanter in drafting and then passing the Judiciary Act of 1925. This important legislation reduced the workload of the Supreme Court, giving it wide latitude on what it would and would not hear. Taft also relied on Van Devanter to handle the details in the construction of the new Supreme Court building in 1935.

While Van Devanter was highly regarded in the court, he became a focus of enmity and frustration outside of it. Following the construction of the Supreme Court building, the nation was in the throes of the Great Depression. In 1932, newly elected president Franklin D. Roosevelt instituted his New Deal to alleviate the people's suffering, stabilize the economy and get people back to work. FDR launched many significant initiatives that radically altered the role of government for business and private individuals. Van Devanter and other justices on the Supreme Court, however, saw significant problems with these new programs and feared government overreach.

For the next four and a half years, Justices Willis Van Devanter, James Clark McReynolds, Pierce Butler and George Sutherland unified in their opposition to Roosevelt's New Deal programs and became publicly known as the Four Horsemen. Together they supported traditional notions of liberty over the pressing demands of "necessity" that many of FDR's programs represented. Roosevelt and his proponents were outraged when the four justices declared the National Recovery Act unconstitutional because it gave the president too much lawmaking power. They also struck down the Railroad Pension Law, the National Recovery Administration and the Agricultural Adjustment Act and ignored complaints that more than 1,600 injunctions by lower courts kept acts of Congress from being enforced. The president, Congress and many critics howled at the injustice of the Supreme Court. They frequently complained that despite Roosevelt winning his reelection by more than 10 million votes and Democrats controlling three-quarters of Congress, their efforts for the benefit of the people were in danger of standing or falling on the votes of only six Supreme Court justices.

On February 5, 1937, Franklin D. Roosevelt asked Congress to increase the number of justices on the Supreme Court. He argued that this move

Willis Van Devanter in
his official judge's robes.
*Wyoming State Archives,
Department of State Parks
and Cultural Resources.*

would increase the efficiency of the court, and he explained that Van Devanter and others had for decades struck down government attempts to help the people, that they "let new facts be blurred through old glasses, fitted as it were, for the needs of another generation." The American public and good portions of Congress balked at this radical change. It was blatantly obvious that Roosevelt intended to pack the court with new justices that would override the opposition of the Four Horsemen and clear the way for his projects.

Ultimately, the issue evaporated when the Supreme Court decided to support an effort by the states to pass minimum wage laws and upheld the National Labor Relations Act, regulating disputes between labor and capital. This unexpected show of support for programs in the New Deal released a great deal of pressure to change the Supreme Court.

The issue was further resolved when Willis Van Devanter announced that he would finally retire on June 21, 1937, after having served on the Supreme

Court for twenty-six years. Van Devanter's years of public service had brought significant legal acumen to the young Wyoming territory. Through savvy political alliances, he ascended to the highest levels of government within Wyoming and just as quickly climbed into the role as a justice of the U.S. Supreme Court.

Willis Van Devanter died on February 28, 1941. He was buried at Cheyenne's Historic Lakeview Cemetery near his great friend and benefactor, Francis E. Warren.

The Van Devanter sculpture was donated by the daughters of William Vines, who graduated from the University of Wyoming Law School in 1966 and practiced law for fifty-one years. Because of their father's background and his love for the law, his daughters chose to honor their father and to recognize the legal profession's impact on Wyoming.

The plaque reads, "Justice Willis Van Devanter by Joel Turner. First person from Wyoming to sit on the United States Supreme Court. In honor of William H. Vines, pillar of our strength. Donated by his daughters Kimberly, Hillary, Jennifer, and Stephanie 2022."

THERESE JENKINS

Location: Northwest corner of Capitol Avenue and 22nd Street
Artist: Joel Turner
Donor: Presbyterian Church

The bronze statue honoring Therese Jenkins stands near the First Presbyterian Church, where she was a member for many years. Jenkins was active in the women's suffrage movement and played a pivotal role in upholding the right of women to vote and the inclusion of the clause in Wyoming's constitution.

When the territorial legislature met in 1889 for the constitutional convention in Cheyenne, there were some delegates opposed to the inclusion clause granting women the right to vote. Therese Jenkins boarded the horse and buggy driven by her husband, James, and they drove through the streets of Cheyenne to rally women to hurry to the capitol to protest the resolution to remove women's voting rights. The women were successful in their protest, and the right for women to vote was included in the Wyoming Constitution. Meanwhile, Therese returned to her home to give birth to her daughter, Agnes Wyoming Jenkins.

Therese Alberta
Jenkins memorial.
*Starley Talbott
photograph.*

Because of Jenkins's effort to save women's suffrage for the new state of Wyoming, she was invited to deliver the keynote address at the statehood celebration on July 23, 1890. She wrote and memorized her speech and then practiced the speech on the steps of the capitol while James and baby Agnes drove off in the buggy, signaling when Therese could be heard and understood. On the day of official celebration, her words rang out loud and clear, ending with these words:

> *And may that beautiful bow of color which spanned our eastern boundary at the golden sunset hour of July 10, 1890, be but a faint promise of the prosperity, the stability, the harmony of our magnificent domain, guided (not governed) by the hand of man clasped in the hand of woman.*

Therese Jenkins continued her service to the community of Cheyenne and the state of Wyoming. In 1892, she attended the Republican National Convention in Minneapolis. In 1893, she spoke in Denver and other Colorado towns in a campaign for a referendum on women's suffrage in support of Colorado becoming the second state in the nation to grant women the right to vote. She attended the convention of the National American Woman's Suffrage Association in 1919.

Jenkins's great-granddaughter Paula Qualls of Cheyenne has numerous anecdotal memories of her famous ancestor. "I never met my great-grandmother Therese, but stories of her community service have inspired me to admire her. She was deeply involved in the Presbyterian Church, and she believed in supporting the rights of women. One time the minister was delivering a sermon that included comments that women should not be exercising their rights such as voting. My great-grandmother stuck her tongue out at the minister who observed her actions. Shortly thereafter, the elders voted to 'church' her and ordered that she could not attend services for several weeks," Paula related.

Jenkins was also involved with the temperance movement. After her husband's death, and when she was unable to walk on her own, she lived with her daughter Agnes Wyoming and Agnes's husband, Carl Metcalf. "Carl liked to drink beer, which did not meet with great-grandmother's approval. One day when Carl was at work and no one else was home, Therese heard a loud popping noise coming from the basement, and she told Carl about it when he came home. He told her would find out what happened and came back to report that it was only the caps popping off the bottles of the root beer he was making," Paula said.

Qualls also said that Jenkins was a prolific writer and interested in education. She established a reading room in a vacant office in a building on Carey Avenue, where she hoped the adults in Cheyenne would spend time reading rather than visiting a saloon.

Several generations of the Jenkins family were present and were honored at a formal dedication of the Jenkins statue on June 25, 2023, at the First Presbyterian Church. Master of ceremonies Dave Cook and Pastor Bob Thompson presided. Many people were recognized and thanked for their participation in the process of supporting the placing of the Jenkins sculpture near the church. Special thanks were given to the sculpture committee, which included Larry Barttelbort, Mary Throne, Greta Morrow, Maida Wedell and Dave Cook.

Left: Paula Qualls admires a clay mold for the statue of her great-grandmother Therese Alberta Jenkins. *Starley Talbott photograph.*

Below: Representatives of *Votes for Women*, giving a presentation at the dedication of the Therese Alberta Jenkins sculpture. *From left*: Keren Meister Emerich, Debra Lee, Mary Guthrie and Rosalind Schliske. *Starley Talbott photograph.*

A special presentation from the acting troupe A League of Her Own, sponsored by the Cheyenne League of Women Voters, honored Jenkins and her advocacy of "Votes for Women." The troupe included Debra Lee, Rosalind Schliske, Mary Guthrie and Keren Meister-Emerich. Lee portrayed Therese Jenkins.

Because of Jenkins's devotion to the First Presbyterian Church in Cheyenne, the members sponsored the bronze statue in her honor. The pedestal for the statue is composed of the same materials used in an addition to the church in 2022. The plaque on back of the statue reads:

> *Born in Madison, Wisconsin, May 1, 1853. Arrived in Cheyenne 1877. Orator at Statehood Ceremony 1890.*
>
> *First woman delegate to a Republican National Convention in 1892.*
>
> *Died February 18, 1936. Interred at Lakeview Cemetery, Cheyenne.*

Family records showed Therese was appalled at the numerous saloons and dance halls in Cheyenne. According to her daughter Agnes Wyoming Jenkins, she responded by focusing on civil welfare and education and improving the social status of women. She was best known as a dedicated temperance worker and a leading advocate for women's suffrage.

Therese's strength of character, ability to stand up to those in power and move others to action and gift as a fine orator made her a leader for women's suffrage.

In 1889, her determined efforts at the Wyoming Constitutional Convention ensured that the new constitution retained women's right to vote, first extended to Wyoming women in 1869.

In the male-dominated society of the 1890s, Therese used her oratory at the statehood festivities on July 23, 1890, as an opportunity to celebrate women's suffrage. Most deemed her address as the most forceful and eloquent one of the day.

Therese and her husband, James, were active in First Presbyterian Church of Cheyenne, contributing their time, talent and treasure to the congregation's work.

As of 2023, six generations of the descendants of Therese A. Jenkins have been baptized at First Presbyterian Church.

AVIATOR

Location: Southwest corner of Capitol Avenue and 22ⁿᵈ Street
Artist: George Lundeen
Donors: Edward F. Murray III and Caren Murray

In 1911, the desire to reach the skies gripped the people of Wyoming. In Cheyenne, a young carpenter, Guy Stoddard, built his own airplane based on French designs he studied and parts he purchased from the sale of pigs. His flying machine was ready by March, and the Cheyenne Frontier Days™ Committee was eager to allow the young airman to make his first attempt at flight from the CFD arena. Unfortunately, security was lax, and vandals damaged his aircraft beyond use when it was left overnight prior to the planned demonstration. While this was a terrible beginning for Wyoming aviation, the enthusiasm of its people was undimmed.

Across the state, an unofficial competition was underway, with several men vying to be the first to fly in Wyoming's skies. Amateur pilots like W.S. Adams of Riverton, A.J. Robinson of Sheridan and Harold Brinker of Cheyenne rushed to complete their machines, even though none had a good grasp on how to control them once they left the ground. The first man to fly over Wyoming was George E. Thompson, a pilot for the Denver Matthewson Biplane Company, by flying a demonstration over Gillette on July 4, 1911. Others soon followed and, overcoming inexperience, introduced Wyoming's people to the wonders of flight.

The First World War distracted many of Wyoming's citizens, and only a few kept flying. Rapid developments during the war overshadowed what had come before, and the flimsy motorized kites that passed for airplanes before were superseded by powerful, sleek, new machines that fought for all sides during the conflict. After the war, aviation returned in earnest, and bold new propositions began to change aviation, and Wyoming's place in it, forever.

In 1919, General Billy Mitchell sought a demonstration that would prove the viability of the airplane in defense of the nation. In September, he and his officers conceived a plan to hold the Air Reliability and Endurance Test. This fantastic affair would bring the best pilots in the Army Air Service into a competition to be the first to fly from one coast to the other and back again, using the most advanced aircraft developed during the war. For this to happen, a route had to be determined and landing sites secured so that aviators piloting these powerful, yet primitive, craft could land, refuel, repair and rest. The officers determined that the best course from Chicago to San Francisco lay along the Union Pacific Railroad, which had already found the shortest route, and additionally found the easiest pass through the Rocky Mountains west of Cheyenne. Arrangements were made, and the first pilots of the contest arrived at a new airfield at Fort D.A. Russell in early October. For the next month, the people of the nation pored over news about these daring flyers who braved mechanical difficulty, a lack of wayfinding equipment and treacherous weather to prove that flight across the nation was possible. Wyoming, considered by all to be the most dangerous portion of the country in which to fly, saw a series of crashes and one fatality as weather and the rugged terrain took their toll.

While many questioned whether flying across America was worth the risk, at least one man saw an opportunity. Otto Praeger, the assistant postmaster general, was delighted at the demonstration. Always an advocate for incorporating technology into the delivery of the mail, he saw the airplane as the next great innovation to get mail speedily across the nation. In 1920, he launched a campaign to establish permanent airfields along the route that General Mitchell's test had identified. Two such airfields were in Wyoming: one at Rock Springs and the other, serving as the division headquarters for the route between North Platte and Salt Lake City, at Cheyenne.

On the early morning of September 8, 1920, the first mail plane piloted by Buck Heffron landed at Cheyenne heading west. The next day, the first mail plane heading east piloted by Jimmy Murray landed. Murray returned on September 13 with a full load of mail, being the first pilot to complete an airmail circuit to Wyoming, thus cementing the first operational aviation circuit in the history of the Rocky Mountain region. For the next six years, bold pilots like Heffron and Murray flew the airmail in all types of weather across Wyoming's rugged terrain.

The planes these pioneer pilots flew were open-cockpit remnants from the Great War. They had no radios, they had no heat and they had no weather reports. Instruments were primitive at best, so pilots navigated the landscape by landmarks or, should they be obscured, by deductive or "dead" reckoning based on calculations of speed, wind direction and time to know where they were going. It took steady nerves to challenge Wyoming, as pilots had to fly higher to get over summits than at any other point in their flights. Aircraft could fail at any time and frequently did. Ranchers and farmers along the route began to know these pilots by name, as they were common visitors to their rural homesteads, awaiting rescue or just asking for a ride to the next train station.

Right: The *Aviator* memorial.
Starley Talbott photograph.

Below: A plaque on the base
of the *Aviator* statue, honoring
airmail pilots. *Starley Talbott
photograph.*

Wyoming made veterans out of the many pilots that ventured through her skies. Jimmy Murray was one of the first, and he was followed by other legendary pilots like Slim Lewis, who flew more miles than nearly any man alive, or Jack Knight, who was the first man to complete a flight across the country at night, doing so in one of the worst winter storms of the twentieth century. Later, Elrey Jeppesen, an airmail pilot who kept excellent records of landmarks and routes he flew across the country, flew out of Cheyenne as well. He eventually created a company making flying charts used by pilots the world over. Jimmy Murray finished his career as the record holder of the most hours flown by any of the airmail pilots. He went on to study law, became vice-president of the Boeing Aircraft Company and worked as a lobbyist in Washington, D.C.

Flying in those early days was a family business for the Murrays. Jimmy was followed by his brother Edward F. Murray Sr., who was also a pilot and remained in Cheyenne, where he founded the insurance agency, Ed Murray & Sons. A third brother, Lawrence, came to Cheyenne as an airplane mechanic, making sure that both of his brothers were as safe as could be.

George Lundeen's statue is dedicated to the Murrays and other brave pilots who challenged the skies around and over Wyoming's Rocky Mountains. They were true pioneers who charted a new path across the West and blazed a trail for all future aviators to follow.

Donors Edward F. Murray III and Caren Murray sponsored the sculpture to honor Ed's grandfather Edward F. Murray Sr. and great-uncle James P. "Jimmy" Murray, who were among the first ever U.S. airmail pilots.

NATIVE GIRL

Location: Northeast corner of Capitol Avenue and 22nd Street
Artist: George Lundeen
Donor: Alice's Lakeside Legacy 2022

The sculpture titled *Native Girl* is a smaller replica of a portion of the sculpture *On the Trail of Discovery* at the Great Plains Art Museum, Lincoln, Nebraska. The statue in Cheyenne represents a Native girl who may have been one of the many Natives encountered by Lewis and Clark during their Corps of Discovery journey.

A sculpture of *Native Girl*, holding an American flag. *Starley Talbott photograph.*

Sculptor George Lundeen, who grew up in Nebraska, created several life-size models of the Lewis and Clark Expedition for the sculpture *On the Trail of Discovery* because he said it represents part of Nebraska's history. The Nebraska exhibit contains statues of Meriwether Lewis and his Newfoundland dog, Seaman; a map held by William Clark; and two statues of Natives, including the life-size statue of a Native girl holding the American flag.

The inscription for the Nebraska sculpture reads, "As Meriwether Lewis and William Clark wound their way westward, they encountered many indigenous people. The Native Americans portrayed here represent those who helped Lewis and Clark during their travel to the Pacific Ocean. The flag that the child is holding and the Thomas Jefferson medal were gifts given to those original people of America."

Lundeen said his research shows that the members of the Corps of Discovery often presented gifts to people they met along the way, and the young girl depicted holding the flag may have been presented the flag as a gift.

The plaque on the Cheyenne sculpture reads, "Native Girl by George Lundeen. Dedicated to all the Native People who cared for the land before it was Wyoming. Donated by Alice's Lakeside Legacy 2022."

Garden Angel

Location: South Side of 22nd Street between Central Avenue and Capitol Avenue
Artist: Julie Jones-Denkers
Donor: John Lee

The *Garden Angel* bronze sculpture provides a calm and peaceful presence near St. Mary's Cathedral in Cheyenne. This statue was chosen by John Lee and his children to honor the life of his wife, Jackie Lee.

John Lee learned of the Capitol Avenue Bronze Project through an online notice and contacted Nathaniel Trelease, project chairman, and Harvey Deselms, curator, to inquire about contributing to the artistic project. Lee didn't have anything in mind for a statue, but he and his son, Chris, and daughter, Amanda, visited the Deselms Fine Art Gallery to discuss possible endeavors. As they browsed through the gallery, Amanda discovered the completed bronze of an angel she thought would be a lovely tribute for her mother, and John and Chris agreed.

Since the *Garden Angel* bronze statue was already completed, as soon as a pedestal was finished, the statue was installed in January 2022 near St. Mary's Cathedral, where the Lee family worshiped.

John Lee and his future wife, Jackie, both grew up in Hornell, New York. They knew each other through school activities and married in 1977. John graduated from the State University of New York at Syracuse University with a degree in environmental science and forestry. He began his career with the Bureau of Land Management. Lee spent thirty-nine years with the BLM doing surveys of boundaries of federal lands. His work took him to Oregon, California, Colorado, Wyoming and Washington, D.C.

The Lees moved to Cheyenne in 1989, where John completed his work with the BLM and Jackie performed clerical work. They both enjoyed the community, volunteer opportunities and travel. Jackie died in 2021.

The *Garden Angel* sculpture, in memory of a loved one. *Starley Talbott photograph.*

John Lee has continued many of his volunteer duties, including assisting with the records division at the office of the Laramie County Sheriff and teaching a basic pistol class. He is also active at St. Mary's Cathedral and Knights of Columbus. A new activity that is providing joy to Lee is participating in the "Miles of Smiles" project. Volunteers take residents of assisted living facilities on three-wheeler bicycle rides.

Travel is another favorite activity for Lee. He is a member of the Cheyenne Chapter of Friendship Force, hosting visits and homestays for folks from all over the world. He has also traveled to many states and countries in conjunction with Friendship Force. He is also a member of several recreational vehicle clubs and travels frequently with these groups.

John Lee and his children are happy to have contributed to the Capitol Avenue Bronze Project with a comforting statue.

The plaque reads, "Garden Angel, by Julie Jones-Denkers. In Loving Memory of Jackie Lee. Resting in an Eternal Garden Surrounded by Flowers, Blue Birds and Cardinals. Dearly Loved and Dearly Missed. 'Your Wings Were Ready, but Our Hearts Were Not.' 2022."

PROMISE OF THE PRAIRIE

Location: Southeast corner of Capitol Avenue and 22ⁿᵈ Street
Artist: George Lundeen
Donors: Drs. Robert Prentice and Sandra Surbrugg

Promise of the Prairie depicts a pioneer family who have arrived in the American West ready to start their new lives as homesteaders. The original sculpture was created by George Lundeen and stands in North Park in Holdrege, Nebraska, the hometown of Lundeen. The statue was placed in Holdrege on June 19, 1983, to commemorate the centennial of the town.

The Homestead Act of 1862 allowed a family to obtain up to 160 acres of land free from the federal government to establish a farm provided they lived on the land for at least five years and could show that they had improved the land. The Homestead Act of 1909 allowed farmers to obtain 320 acres of free land. The allotment was increased again in 1916 to 640 acres. In 1912, the homestead residence requirement was lowered from five years to three years.

Large numbers of people took advantage of the Homestead Acts to establish farms in several states, including Nebraska and Wyoming. Beginning in 1912, more than 100,000 acres of land were claimed by homesteaders

The *Promise of the Prairie* sculpture, depicting a young farm family. *Starley Talbott photograph.*

75

in Laramie County, Wyoming. The years of 1913 and 1914 brought more expansion of farmland to the area.

The Capitol Avenue sculpture *Promise of the Prairie* is a copy of the original sculpture by George Lundeen. Lundeen envisioned the statue to represent "the spirit of the pioneer."

The plaque on the sculpture in Cheyenne reads, "Promise of the Prairie by George Lundeen. In honor of the families past and present who have made Wyoming home. Drs. Robert Prentice & Sandra Surbrugg 2021."

PRIORITY MAIL

Location: Northwest corner of Capitol Avenue and 21ˢᵗ Street
Artist: Bobbie Carlyle
Donors: Multiple

Before the official launch of the Capitol Avenue Bronze Project, a few bronze sculptures had been placed on Capitol Avenue. One of these early statues was *Priority Mail* by bronze artist Bobbie Carlyle.

Carlyle expressed her thoughts on creating this bronze in these words: "Ask both young and old and they will tell you that receiving mail is a treat. The anticipation of finding out what the mail will bring fills us with excitement and wonder. These four children wait around and on top of the mailbox, anticipating the arrival of the mail. Could it be a letter from Grandma, their older brother, or their pen pal across the country?"

A long list of donors contributed to the *Priority Mail* sculpture.

The *Priority Mail* sculpture, depicting children checking a mailbox. *Starley Talbott photograph.*

FAMILY TIES

Location: Southwest Corner of Capitol Avenue and 21ˢᵗ Street
Artist: Chris Navarro
Donors: Dixie and Tom Roberts

The sculpture *Family Ties* depicts the bond between a brother and sister along with the importance of connections between family members. The statue shows a big brother bending down on his knees, tying the shoelaces of his little sister. He is protective, and he is looking after her and making sure she is safe, while she looks down on him with a smile.

The sculptor, Chris Navarro, says that this sculpture reminds us of the importance of the incredible bond between siblings. He added that this angelic scene would make any mom or dad proud of the love and protection shown by a brother toward his sister.

Donors Dixie and Tom Roberts are proud to sponsor the statue in honor of their own "family ties." The plaque reads, "Family Ties by Chris Navarro.

The *Family Ties* sculpture, depicting the bond between a brother and a sister. *Starley Talbott photograph.*

With Love and Devotion to Adam, Helen and John Roberts; and to Dorothy and Vernon Sims, Gary, Rhonda and Wanda. Donated by Dixie and Tom Roberts 2022."

IN GOOD HANDS

Location: Northeast corner of Capitol Avenue and 21ˢᵗ Street
Artist: Robin Laws
Donor: Nathaniel T. Trelease

The sculpture *In Good Hands* was chosen by Nathaniel T. Trelease, chairman of the Capitol Avenue Bronze Commission, and his family to honor his mother, Ceralia Solis. The statue stands in front of the Cathedral of St. Mary, the 116-year-old Gothic church that has for generations been the home church of the family.

Sculptor Robin Laws created the statue of an angel watching over several animals that were created from memories of some of Robin's favorite pets, all of whom she names and all of whom she misses. The angel embraces a cat, Della, while the other animal are gathered around the angel's feet. They include a donkey, Jennifer; a dog, Puff; and a bunny, Buck.

The *In Good Hands* sculpture, depicting animals in the good hands of an angel. *Starley Talbott photograph.*

The capstone on which the pedestal rests is unique among the capstones and pedestals in the bronze project. Don Jones, the master mason who worked on the renovation of the capitol and is also the mason of the bronze project, had a small amount of sandstone left over from the capitol renovation. He fashioned that sandstone into the capstone for *In Good Hands*.

Trelease stated that all creatures in his mother's care, especially her children, were always in good hands. He hopes that the bronze legacy sculptures have similarly been in good hands.

The plaque reads, "In Good Hands by Robin Laws. In loving memory of our mother Ceralia Solis and her lifelong example of hope, faith, and love. Nathaniel T. Trelease, Joyce Solis, Patricia Solis Dolbey, and Kimberly Tregilgas 2021."

MARY O'HARA

Location: Southeast corner of Capitol Avenue and 21ˢᵗ Street
Artist: Joel Turner
Donors: Family of Carol McMurry

The rugged Remount Ranch west of Cheyenne, Wyoming, provided the backdrop for Mary O'Hara's beloved books about ranching and horses. Her best-known novels are *My Friend Flicka, Thunderhead* and *Green Grass of Wyoming.*

O'Hara and her husband, Helge Sture-Vasa, purchased a ranch near Cheyenne in 1930 and named it Remount Ranch. Helge brought his experience of working with horses in the U.S. Army Remount Service to the property in Wyoming. The ranch played a historic role, in the late 1800s, of exchanging horses with the U.S. Cavalry on its way to and from Fort D.A. Russell. The traded animals were called remount horses, thus providing the name for the ranch.

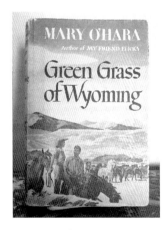

The cover of *Green Grass of Wyoming*, written by Mary O'Hara. *Starley Talbott photograph.*

"When we moved to Wyoming, it was a great change. Wyoming impressed me more deeply than any other place I have lived. There is such emptiness, such solitude, such vastness," O'Hara said in a quote from the May 28, 1952 edition of the *Wyoming State Tribune.*

O'Hara took an active part in running the ranch, where she helped with the animals and often cooked for both guests and employees. At one time, she ran a dairy and delivered milk to customers in Cheyenne. The couple raised sheep, a few cattle and horses. They experienced economic hardship during the Depression. To add income during this difficult time, O'Hara began writing Wyoming ranch

The Mary O'Hara
memorial. *Starley
Talbott photograph.*

stories. Her first novel, *My Friend Flicka*, created the life of a young boy and
his horse on the high plains of Wyoming. The sequels, *Thunderhead* and
Green Grass of Wyoming, carried on the legacy of the McLaughlin family. She
published nine books from 1930 to 1982. Her books were so popular that
they were translated into many languages, and some were made into movies.

The Remount Ranch was sold in 1946, and Mary and Helge moved to
California. O'Hara had previously worked as a Hollywood screenwriter
during the silent film era. She was also an accomplished pianist and composer.
Mary and Helge divorced in 1947, and she moved to Connecticut and later
to Maryland, where she lived until her death in 1980.

The family of Carol McMurry, who was a librarian, honored her memory
with the sculpture of Mary O'Hara. The plaque reads, "Mary O'Hara
Author, by Joel Turner. Given in memory of Carol McMurry by her family,
Paul and Carla Bankes; Matt and Stephanie Seebaum; and Pat Spiels, 2022."

George Rainsford

Location: Northwest corner of Capitol Avenue and 20ᵗʰ Street
Artist: Joel Turner
Donors: Ibby and Rick Davis

The statue of George Rainsford stands a few blocks west of an area in Cheyenne known as the Rainsford Historic District. Rainsford was a prominent architect and designed many of the homes in the area from Warren Avenue on the west, 25ᵗʰ Street on the north, 16ᵗʰ Street on the south and Morrie Avenue on the east.

Rainsford moved from New York to Wyoming in 1879. He established a ranch west of Chugwater, Wyoming, around 1881, where he raised livestock. On his Diamond Ranch, Rainsford earned national and international renown for his fine Morgan and Thoroughbred horses.

Trained as an architect and civil engineer when he lived in New York, Rainsford left his mark on many buildings in Cheyenne. He designed his "city house" in Cheyenne at 702 East 18ᵗʰ Street. Many of Cheyenne's wealthy ranchers maintained homes in Cheyenne in the late 1800s. Rainsford's home differed from others in the neighborhood because he attached the stables to the mansion, as was done in the eastern United States. The home was a frame house with a sharp mansard roof and set-in porches under rounded domes. He soon designed other homes of the era for the cattle barons and prominent residents in Cheyenne.

The area containing many of Rainsford's buildings, about thirty square blocks of the original city of Cheyenne, is designated a National Historic Site and described on the nomination form in these words:

> *Rainsford is best known for his experiments with varieties of roof shapes and simplified traditional styles. His influence and that of the eclectic vitality of the age is visible throughout the district, reflected in multiple roof and dormer shapes, ornamental windows with tracery, stained, leaded, beveled and etched glass and in an abundance of machine produced ornaments on porches, bay windows, and gable ends, nineteenth-century American equivalents of European folk art.*

Some of the homes designed by Rainsford include the R.S. Van Tassell home at 921 East 17ᵗʰ, the Charles Potter home at 1722 Warren Avenue, the Amasa R. Converse home at 118 East 18ᵗʰ and the Samuel Corson home at

George Rainsford
memorial. *Starley Talbott
photograph.*

209 East 18th. One of his most prominent buildings was the Cheyenne Club at 120 East 17th Street.

Rainsford's Diamond Ranch was sold in 1922 along with his Cheyenne house. He returned to New York, where he divided his time between New York City and Daytona Beach, Florida. He died in 1935.

Dr. Rick Davis and Ibby Davis are the donors of the Rainsford bronze sculpture. They are longtime supporters of the arts in Cheyenne. They decided to sponsor the Rainsford statue because Ibby's father, Russell Potter, was chairman of the department of architecture at Miami University from 1933 to 1947.

Wyoming, Ohio, is the original home of both Rick Davis and Ibby Potter. They met in kindergarten, fell in love in seventh grade and eventually married in 1962. Rick graduated from the University of Cincinnati with a degree in medicine, specializing in cardiology. Ibby graduated from Goucher College in Maryland with a degree in art history and earned a teaching degree from Miami University in Oxford, Ohio.

Dr. Davis was sent to Francis E. Warren Air Force Base in Cheyenne in 1969 for a two-year tour of duty as a doctor at the base. The couple found it hard to find housing, as the base was a busy place at that time. Eventually, they were housed on the base in Quarter One on officers' row.

Cheyenne was a welcoming city, and the Davises decided to stay in the city. Dr. Davis was a cardiologist at the Internal Medicine Group from 1973 to 2009. He also served on the hospital staff and was a part-time teacher for the University of Wyoming medical school.

Ibby is an artist in her own right, has taught watercolor classes at Laramie County Community College and has attended an advanced painting class at LCCC for thirty-eight years. She has exhibited and sold many of her paintings throughout the community. Both Ibby and Rick have served on many volunteer boards in Cheyenne, including the Old West Museum, the Cheyenne Symphony, the Children's Society and many others.

An opportunity for Ibby came when she was asked to be ombudsman in the office of Governor Mike Sullivan, where she ended up serving for eight years. The Davises traveled to Ireland to visit the governor when he served as ambassador there.

One of Dr. Davis's proudest moments was serving as a doctor aboard three honor flights for World War II veterans. He contacted each Wyoming veteran who went on one of the flights prior to departure for Washington, D.C.

Both Dr. Davis and Ibby Davis treasure a photo of Governor Mike Sullivan and First Lady Jane Sullivan signed with these words from the governor: "Ibby and Rick, You have been a little bit of everything to us and we are grateful. But, Ibby, for the joy and inspiration you have provided to so many and for the example you have set for those young people we have watched mature, we are full of respect and admiration."

The plaque reads, "George Rainsford by Joel Turner. We dedicate this sculpture to George Rainsford and his architectural accomplishments, but just as importantly to all people of Cheyenne who have enhanced the charm and character of our small prairie town on the northern plains. The visual arts have added not only refinement and grace, but also inspire lasting pride in the Queen City of the plains. Rick and Ibby Davis 2023."

CHIEF YELLOW CALF

Location: Southwest corner of Capitol Avenue and 20th Street
Artist: Tanner Loren
Donor: American National Bank

Chief Yellow Calf served as the last chief of the Northern Arapaho tribe in Wyoming. He was born a few years before the Treaty of 1868, by which the Northern Arapaho Tribe was assigned to land in the Wind River Indian Reservation in west-central Wyoming. Chief Yellow Calf lived from 1861 to 1938 and is considered one of the Northern Arapaho tribe's most important and respected leaders in its history. He earned the honor to be called "Last to Lead His People."

Sculptor Tanner Loren conducted extensive research regarding typical Northern Arapaho beadwork patterns and headdresses made from eagle feathers. His image of Yellow Calf is based on photographs and information provided by descendants.

Descendants of the chief's family still reside on Wyoming's Wind River Reservation. Loren was fortunate to meet with members of the family, including Matt Wallowing Bull.

Chief Yellow Calf memorial.
Starley Talbott photograph.

Loren was invited to participate in a Sweat Lodge Ceremony featuring the performance of traditional songs. "That was an experience I will forever treasure," he said.

Chief Yellow Calf is depicted holding a peace pipe because he was oriented toward peaceful relations with the U.S. government. He is shown wearing a full-length blanket to convey his need for protection against the elements and the possible uncertainties of the times.

The American National Bank sponsored the statue to signify a commitment to downtown Cheyenne and the community.

The plaque reads, "Chief Yellow Calf by Tanner Loren. In honor of Chief Yellow Calf, who was a Northern Arapaho religious leader and member of the Arapaho Shoshone Joint Business Council. He is remembered for his preservation of religious practices and his advocacy of equal rights for Indigenous people. Donated by ANB Bank 2022."

Joseph E. Stimson

Location: Northeast corner of Capitol Avenue and 20ᵗʰ Street
Artist: Joel Turner
Donor: Greg Dykeman

Joseph Stimson's bronze statue is facing south on Capitol Avenue toward Stimson's former photography studio and the Union Pacific Railroad Depot. As a photographer, Stimson used his camera to capture a visual concept of Cheyenne and Wyoming during a transitional time in history.

Stimson arrived in Cheyenne at the age of nineteen in 1889 and established a photography studio on Capitol Avenue. He worked primarily as a studio portrait photographer for a decade, and he photographed his future bride, Anna Peterson, whom he married in 1894. In 1904, the couple moved to the house that Joseph built at 214 West 25ᵗʰ Street north of the capitol.

Wyoming's state engineer, Elwood Mead, offered Stimson the opportunity to travel throughout Wyoming and photograph Wyoming's scenic beauty. Mead and Stimson spent the summer of 1895 in the Big Horn Mountains, where Stimson became captivated by the majesty of the mountains. He later photographed the Teton Mountains, Jackson and the Yellowstone area.

Stimson's scenic photos caught the attention of a publicist for the Union Pacific Railroad, and in 1901, he was hired by the railroad to document all facets of the railroad. He eventually captured on film the natural wonders, towns and cities, farms and ranches, irrigation systems, reclamation projects, mines and industry, as well as the tracks, depots, trains and personnel of the Union Pacific.

In 1904, Stimson was hired to produce photos for an exhibit at the Louisiana Purchase Exposition in St. Louis. He earned a silver medal for the exhibit and went on to produce another exhibit at the Lewis and Clark Exposition in Portland, Oregon, in 1905, earning another silver medal.

Throughout his career as a photographer, Stimson photographed Cheyenne's people, streets, buildings, homes, businesses and churches. He recorded the city's first Frontier Days™ celebration in 1897. Unfortunately, many of Stimson's early studio portraits were lost after a shelf collapsed in the basement of his home near the capitol, breaking a number of glass plates holding those photographs.

However, luckily for the citizens of Wyoming, Stimson's photographic collection of more than eight thousand glass plates and nitrate negatives spanning half a century of work were saved and retained. The collection

Left: Joseph E. Stimson memorial. *Starley Talbott photograph.*

Below: The former home of photographer Joseph E. Stimson, previously located north of the Wyoming Capitol. *J.E. Stimson Collection, Wyoming State Archives, Department of State Parks and Cultural Resources.*

is housed at the Wyoming State Archives, Museums and Historical Department in Cheyenne.

Fond memories of Joseph and Anna Stimson remain with their great-granddaughter Kim Patterson Mill, who resides in Cheyenne. "Even though I never met my great-grandfather Joseph Stimson, family members always called him 'Daddy Joe,' so I also refer to him by that name," she said.

Joseph and Anna Stimson were the parents of two daughters: Louise, born in 1895, and Josephine, born in 1905. An infant daughter, Catherine, died in 1910. Both Louise and Josephine attended school in Cheyenne. Josephine served as an assistant librarian in the Carnegie Library in Cheyenne before moving away.

Louise married Richard Alexander Patterson I, and they had one son named Richard Alexander Patterson II. They lived in several states before moving to Cheyenne, where Louise's husband, Richard Patterson, died in 1931, when their son was only six years old. Louise's mother, Anna, died in 1938.

After attending librarian school, Louise served as a librarian in Cheyenne until 1946. She married Colonel Henry Paul Hallowell, who was stationed at Fort Francis E. Warren in Cheyenne. During World War II, Colonel Hallowell was dispatched to the Philippines, and Louise accompanied him there. His son, Paul, and Louise's son, Richard "Dick" Patterson, stayed with Dick's grandfather Joseph Stimson in the family home on 25th Street north of the Capitol. Paul and Dick went on to serve in World War II, and they returned to attend the University of Wyoming following their military service.

Dick Patterson married Evalyn Bon in 1950, and they became the parents of Richard "Rick" Alexander Patterson III, Kim and Donnica. The family lived in Cheyenne, and the children attended St. Mary's Catholic School. The school was only a block away from the home of their grandmother Louise and the capitol. Louise and Colonel Hallowell had been living in Connecticut when her father, Joseph, visited them and died there in 1952. Colonel Hallowell died in 1956, and Louise moved back to Cheyenne to live in the Stimson family home.

"We would often go to grandmother's home for lunch or after school, and sometimes for dinner. When we ate dinner with Grandmother Louise, after dinner we walked around the capitol building. Grandmother loved to skip, and she taught us to skip, so we often skipped around the capitol," Kim recalled.

Kim Patterson Mill also said that she always enjoyed visiting the Stimson home because the picture window presented a view of the north side of the capitol when there were no other buildings there. She also liked seeing the basement of the home where her great-grandfather Joseph had worked with his photography equipment and where his glass plate negatives were stored. The Stimson home was torn down when the State of Wyoming purchased the property in the area for the expansion of state buildings.

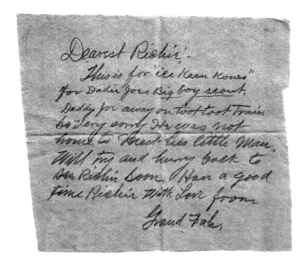

Opposite: Robert A. Patterson II, the grandson of Joseph E. Stimson, photographed in a cowboy outfit. *J.E. Stimson Collection, Wyoming State Archives, Department of State Parks and Cultural Resources.*

Left: A note written by Joseph E. Stimson to his grandson Robert A. Patterson. *Courtesy of Kim Mill, great-granddaughter of J.E. Stimson.*

Kim continues to live in Cheyenne, and she is happy to own many of her "Daddy Joe's" framed photographs, his former work table and his medals won at the Universal Exposition in 1904 and the Lewis and Clark Centennial Exposition in 1905. She also has one of the headlamps from Joseph Stimson's favorite Ford automobile.

Some prints from Joseph Stimson's photos that his great-granddaughter Kim is especially fond of include those of her father, Richard "Dick" Patterson, when he was a child. Joseph photographed him dressed in cowboy attire for the annual rodeo. Dick's grandfather fondly called him "Richie" and wrote a heartwarming note that remains in the family memorabilia.

The Stimson sculpture on Capitol Avenue was donated by Cheyenne attorney Greg Dykeman to honor one of Cheyenne's visionary leaders. Dykeman is a graduate of the University of Wyoming and has contributed many gifts to the university, including the Law School Enrichment Fund.

As an estate attorney, Dykeman has learned that many people feel immense pleasure when they provide a charitable gift to others. "I have learned there is tremendous joy in philanthropy. Every time I make a gift, it makes me smile," Dykeman says. He is proud to support the Capitol Avenue Bronze Legacy with his gift in honor of Wyoming's famous photographer of the West, Joseph Stimson.

The plaque reads, "J.E. Stimson, Renowned Photographer, by Joel Turner. Donated by Gregory C. Dykeman to honor visionary leaders for making our community strong, vibrant, prosperous and beautiful, 2022."

JOHN COLTER

Location: Southeast Corner of Capitol Avenue and 20th Street
Artist: Tanner Loren
Donor: Robert Born

Young John Colter was among the men who set out from St. Louis on the Missouri River with the Lewis and Clark Expedition on May 14, 1804. Colter was a strong man and was prized for his hunting skills on the arduous journey.

The Corps of Discovery, as the expedition was known, included several boats loaded with tons of equipment necessary for the trip, which was to provide a water route across the continent, study the plants and wildlife and make contact with Indigenous people. Members of the group worked long, hard days, often dragging the boats upstream when the current was too strong to paddle. John Colter, tasked with providing meat for the men, set off many days to hunt for wild game. Colter also navigated small streams along the route to provide information about possible obstacles.

Colter was born in Virginia around 1774. He was not interested in farming, and when he was twenty years old, he lived on the frontier in Kentucky and other areas. He made contact with various Native American tribes and learned some sign language. With these skills, Colter was able to communicate with the tribes encountered on the Lewis and Clark journey.

In October 1804, the corps made contact with the members of the Mandan tribe, near the present town of Bismarck, North Dakota. Lewis and Clark decided to spend the winter in the area and established a small fort near the largest Mandan village. During their stay, they met the French trapper Toussaint Charbonneau and his Native American wife, Sacagawea, who agreed to accompany the expedition in the spring of 1805. The corps left on April 7, 1805, and completed the journey over the mountains and down the Columbia River to the Pacific Ocean. The group spent the winter there and began the journey homeward in the spring of 1806.

The corps floated ashore at the familiar Mandan village on August 14, 1806. A few days later, John Colter met with Lewis and Clark to tell them that he wished to join two trappers, Forrest Hancock and Jo Dickson, who planned to head back to the west to trap beaver. Colter was released from his duties with the corps and began the next chapter of his explorations.

Colter and the trappers spent the following winter gathering beaver pelts and making contact with Native Americans. In the spring of 1807, they

John Colter memorial. *Starley Talbott photograph.*

journeyed downstream to sell their wares. At the Mandan village, they met Manuel Lisa, the owner of the Missouri Fur Company. Colter agreed to hire on with Lisa and returned west to work at Fort Remon at the confluence of the Bighorn and Yellowstone Rivers near present-day Billings, Montana.

In October 1807, Colter ventured farther south and west into the territory that would become Wyoming. He set out by himself to trek through the area in the winter to strengthen ties with the Native Americans and assess beaver trapping areas. Colter had become friends with some of the members of the Crow tribe, and he spent some time at their camp near present-day Cody, Wyoming, where he experienced the sights and smells of hot springs. Colter then traveled south through the Absaroka mountains and then west to Jackson Hole, where a portion of Jackson Lake is named Colter Bay. As he journeyed north, he saw parts of Yellowstone and was the first white man to see the area's geothermal marvels. Colter's exact route is not known, but his trek through northwest Wyoming in the winter of 1807 is considered a feat of bravery and endurance.

Colter returned to Fort Remo in the spring of 1808. He then spent two more years plying his trapping trade in the Rocky Mountains. Several fur companies also began employing trappers to work in the area. In 1810, Colter returned east and helped William Clark create a detailed map of the northern Rocky Mountains. He then purchased a farm in Missouri, where he died in 1813.

Donor Robert Born was impressed by Tanner Loren when they met at the Western Spirit Art Show at the Old West Museum in Cheyenne in 2020. Born purchased a small sculpture from Loren for his home.

Robert Born wanted to participate in the Capitol Avenue Bronze Project by donating a sculpture in honor of his friend Elizabeth Escobedo. He did not have anything in particular in mind, but when he learned that a sculpture of John Colter by Tanner Loren was available, he knew that was the statue he would sponsor.

Richard and Elizabeth Escobedo became friends with Robert Born after he moved to Cheyenne in 1971. They shared many common interests, including the Cheyenne Little Theatre, the Cheyenne Frontier Days™ Old West Museum and the Mended Hearts group.

Robert Born enlisted in the Wyoming Air National Guard in 1979 when he was encouraged to do so by Richard Escobedo. Born served in the National Guard for twenty-nine years.

The trio's other common bond was the Mended Hearts group. They shared heart-related medical issues. Liz Escobedo was one of the founding members of Cheyenne's Hearts Afire Chapter 132 of Mended Hearts. The group's mission is to serve as a support group for all cardiac patients. They visit patients, answer questions and have provided several Automated External Defibrillators (AEDs) in the community.

Richard Escobedo died in 1999, and Elizabeth died in 2020. Elizabeth moved to Scottsdale, Arizona, following her husband's death. Robert Born

Opposite: Don Jones, stonemason, and Jake Johnson, president of Harold F. Johnson Masonry, installing the John Colter statue. *Starley Talbott photograph.*

Right: The back of the John Colter statue showing a heart on the hem of Colter's jacket, symbolizing the Mended Hearts organization. *Starley Talbott photograph.*

often spent time in Arizona and continued his friendship with Elizabeth. He wanted to honor her for her years of service in Cheyenne by providing a sculpture in her name. On the back of the sculpture of John Colter is a small heart near the hem of Colter's jacket, a symbol for Mended Hearts.

The plaque reads, "Mountain Man, John Colter, by Tanner Loren. Given to the City of Cheyenne in Memory of Elizabeth (Liz) Escobedo by Robert A. Born, 2022."

SHEEP WAGON

Location: Northwest corner of Capitol Avenue and 19th Street
Artist: Tanner Loren
Donors: Dr. Fred Emerich and Dr. Keren Meister-Emerich

The sheep wagon was often a common sight on the western landscape. It represented an earlier culture and tells the history of a time and place when sheep numbered in the millions in Wyoming.

Cattle dominated the plains of Wyoming in the mid- to late 1800s. The severe winter of 1886–87 killed thousands of cattle in Wyoming. Many of the large cattle barons left the area after the loss of their cattle herds, leaving an opportunity for sheep to be introduced to the range. By 1900, almost 4 million sheep populated Wyoming.

Large ranches made use of the thousands of acres of public lands in Wyoming to graze both cattle and sheep. Cattle could often be left to graze in the summer mountain ranges mostly without constant attention. Sheep required human intervention to maintain the safety of the flocks. Sheepherders were employed to tend the bands of sheep, move them from one grazing area to another and find water for them. The herders bedded the sheep down for the night and kept watch for predators. The herder needed a place to live so he or she could stay close to the flock.

A shelter for the herder needed to be mobile so it could easily follow the sheep to various grazing grounds. The sheep wagon provided a home with a source of heat, a place to cook and a place to rest. Most sheep wagons were about twelve feet long and six feet wide, with a canvas-covered top. It held a stove and lots of storage space, both inside and outside, to hold supplies and supplemental feed. There was bed at the back of the wagon

A typical sheepherder's wagon with a flock of sheep near Glenrock, Wyoming, circa 1935. *Photo by Coyote Smith; Wyoming State Archives, Department of State Parks and Cultural Resources.*

The Harold F. Johnson Masonry Company provided the transportation moving the sheep wagon sculpture to its place on Capitol Avenue. *Starley Talbott photograph.*

and benches along the sides. A table could be slid out from a slot under the bed. The door was usually at the front of the wagon so the herder could drive the wagon hitched to a team of horses. The door on most wagons was a "Dutch door"—the door's top half could remain open while the bottom half could stay shut.

A sheep wagon was often built by the rancher who needed one, a local lumber company or the local blacksmith. A very large sheep operation such as the Warren Livestock Company in Cheyenne often employed blacksmiths who worked full-time at the ranch building and repairing the more than forty sheep wagons on the Warren ranch.

The largest number of sheep on Wyoming ranches was 5,480,000 in 1910; this had dropped to 2,360,000 by 1960. It has steadily declined since that time. A few ranches still use sheep wagons, although most sheep wagons today are seen in museums or have been restored for private use.

Fred and Keren Meister-Emerich are the donors of the bronze sculpture of a sheep wagon on Capitol Avenue in Cheyenne. Fred grew up on a ranch east of Cheyenne, where his family raised both sheep and cattle. Fred said that his family did not have a sheep wagon, but their ranch was bordered on the north by the Warren Livestock Company, which pastured thousands of sheep and owned dozens of sheep wagons.

Emerich's father, Carl, established their ranch in the 1940s and registered their sheep brand, the Bar 44. Fred said that they raised mostly Columbia sheep, and he fondly remembers belonging to 4-H and FFA, where he showed his sheep and other animals at the county fair in Cheyenne. The ranch was sold in 1959, and Carl Emerich worked for a number of years at the Stock Growers National Bank in Cheyenne (now the Wells Fargo Bank).

Fred graduated from East High School in Cheyenne in 1963, the University of Wyoming in 1968 and Colorado State University in 1973, with a doctorate degree in veterinary medicine. He spent several years practicing in other states and then returned to Cheyenne, where he practiced at the Yellowstone Animal Hospital. He also worked for the Wyoming Livestock Board as a food safety inspector.

Both Fred and Keren are involved in various activities in Cheyenne. Keren Meister moved in 1972 from Michigan to Wyoming, where she obtained a master's degree in statistics at the University of Wyoming. She worked at Mountain Bell Telephone Company for a few years and taught computer

The *Sheep Wagon* memorial. *Starley Talbott photograph.*

and technical courses at East High School for twenty years. She met Fred at Cheyenne Frontier Days™ in 1976, and they married in 1978. She earned her Doctorate of Education degree in 2008 and teaches statistics to graduate students online for Walden University. The couple have one daughter and one granddaughter.

The Emerichs are longtime volunteers at Cheyenne Frontier Days™, where Fred served as a veterinarian for thirty years, and Keren currently serves on the Public Relations Committee. Their other commitments to the community include Fred's two terms in the Wyoming State Senate and one term as a Laramie County commissioner and Keren's membership on the boards of the Wyoming Commission on Judicial Conduct and Ethics, the Cheyenne Botanic Gardens and the Wyoming Women's Business Center.

Fred and Keren are thrilled to be the donors of a bronze sculpture created by Tanner Loren, who was happy to adorn *Sheep Wagon* with the Emerich ranch sheep brand, Bar 44.

The plaque reads, "Sheep Wagon, by Tanner Loren. Donated by Dr. Fred Emerich and Dr. Keren Meister-Emerich in memory of Mary (Trostle) Emerich and Carl Emerich. The Bar 44 sheep brand was created in the 1940s and used at their ranch east of Cheyenne. Fred has maintained ownership of the Bar 44 brand since he received it from his father in 1980."

Pump Jack

Location: Southwest corner of Capitol Avenue and 19th Street
Artist: Joey Bainer
Donor: Jonah Bank of Wyoming

The first mention of petroleum in Wyoming's past came from the reports of renowned explorer Captain Benjamin L.E. Bonneville, who came west on the first wagon train to come through Wyoming in the early 1830s. Others who traversed the country on the Oregon Trail or hunted furs reported "oil springs" in a variety of locations. These places were known to Indigenous people of the territory, who had long used the greasy material as medicine or a base for paints.

The first attempt to profit from Wyoming's oil springs happened near present-day Casper in 1863 as entrepreneurs sold the oil as axel lubricant. In 1866, another entrepreneur, John C. Fiere, began packing oil in barrels near

Fort Bridger for use as lubrication on the nearby Union Pacific Railroad. From the same spring, Judge C.M. White began shipping oil to Salt Lake City for use by local tanners in their production of leather.

By the early 1880s, a new oil product, kerosene, was becoming popular for lighting not only in Wyoming but also across the nation. It was demand for this fuel that spurred new drilling near Casper, as well as the Big Horn Basin and southwestern Wyoming. In 1895, a small crude oil refinery was established by Philip Shannon's Pennsylvania Oil and Gas Company at Casper that could produce one hundred barrels of lubricating oil per day. These initial efforts at making oil profitable in Wyoming were small, but big events on the horizon would bring explosive growth.

In 1893, the Duryea brothers introduced the first "horseless carriage" to the American public. This amazing contraption captured the imaginations of many, and developments proceeded swiftly to bring the automobile to the masses. As a result, the demand for gasoline, the preferred fuel for this new mode of transportation, skyrocketed, and Wyoming's oil industry boomed. By 1917, several refineries were in operation in the state, with the plant in Casper, run by Standard Oil, being the largest in the world. The 1920s were the apex of Wyoming's oil production. Even though Wyoming had an early start in the field, its status as an oil state declined as larger and more profitable fields opened elsewhere. Production of oil continued through the twentieth century, suffered continuous boom and bust cycles and was hit particularly hard in the 1970s and 1980s.

While crude oil, kerosene, lubricants and gasoline were common products of Wyoming's oil fields, one product, natural gas, proved particularly difficult to extract and initially had limited value. First commercialized as a fuel source as early as 1785, natural gas nevertheless took a back seat to coal as a preferred source of energy until growing environmental concerns during the late 1960s brought it to the fore as a clean-burning alternative. Wyoming was known to have deep reserves of gas under the Pinedale Anticline in the western part of the state, but the gas was trapped under a deep layer of subterranean sandstone that was difficult if not impossible for contemporary drilling technology to penetrate.

By the 1990s, drilling technology had advanced to the point that releasing natural gas was feasible, though financially risky. Regardless, the McMurry Oil Company decided to take the risk and implement new fracking technology developed by petroleum engineer James Shaw at the Jonah Field south of the Pinedale Anticline in 1991. The new technique, which involved pumping high-pressure liquids into a drilled shaft to crack the dense sandstone, proved incredibly successful. The McMurry Oil Company tried the new system on three wells it had acquired, it found that the fracking process produced 2 million cubic feet of gas each day. The company and its partners scrambled over the next few years to establish pipelines to California. The Jonah Field and the nearby Pinedale Anticline became home to thousands of new, highly productive wells. Through its efforts, the McMurry Oil Company initiated one of the greatest natural gas developments in America during the late twentieth century.

Success brought ever greater attention to the region from big oil companies. In 2000, the Alberta Energy Company purchased the McMurry Oil Company, and a few years later, the McMurry family sold their remaining interests at Jonah Field to Shell Oil.

In 2005, Mick McMurry and John W. Martin decided that proceeds from the sale of the family oil business should be invested in a business designed to benefit the people of Wyoming. Using funds from the sale of their oil business as feeder capital, McMurry and Martin started Jonah Bank, named after the gas field that made their fortune. Opening its first branch in Casper in July 2006, Jonah Bank learned the business of local banking and was deeply involved in community events and projects. In November 2006, the company's success allowed it to open its first branch in Cheyenne. By 2023, Jonah Bank had two banking facilities in both Casper and Cheyenne. Dedicated to helping local citizens, businesses and not-for-profit corporations, Jonah Bank continues to support Wyoming's communities.

Pump Jack depicts a piece of oil field machinery commonly known as the "horse head" pump jack. Unless the oil is gushing out of the ground, it rarely emerges from wells on its own. Early in the history of the oil industry, it was understood that some sort of pumping mechanism was needed to extract the heavy, viscous fluid from the earth. The first pump was a common kitchen hand pump, installed by Edwin L. Drake in Pennsylvania in 1859. As more wells were dug and went deeper, innovative technologies emerged allowing steam engines to replace manpower. In 1875, huge new wooden "walking beams" fastened to a "sampson post" rocked back and forth, pulling large quantities of oil from the ground with each upward swing of the pump end. Iron beams and bars eventually replaced the older wood and rope mechanisms. In 1925, Walter Trout of the Lufkin Foundry and Machine Company sketched a design for a new system made completely from metal. His first "horse head" pump was well suited for the task but took some time to catch on. By 1926, his perfectly balanced machine had become widely accepted and has continued, with various design improvements, to work the

The *Pump Jack* sculpture, a symbol of Wyoming's energy industry. *Starley Talbott photograph.*

world's oil fields ever since. These machines, methodically moving in large groups or in solitary isolation in the remotest corners of our state, are a common sight in Wyoming.

As part of the Capitol Avenue Bronze Project, Jonah Bank determined that the pump jack, a common piece of machinery seen across Wyoming, would stand as an excellent testament to the people who work in Wyoming's oil industry. It also serves as a suitable reminder of the fortune that allowed the bank to come into existence.

Artist Joey Bainer was selected to produce the sculpture after lengthy discussions with Harvey Deselms, curator of the project. Joey is primarily a figurative sculptor, and this piece was not something he had broad experience with. Just the same, he realized that the angular nature of the subject was straightforward, although he did not know the details about what the most dynamic way would be to depict the machine. After consulting with Steve Skaer, a friend in the oil business, Bainer determined that it was best to have the massive head of the pump jack facing down. Skaer explained that if the head was down, it was working. If the head was up, that meant that the pump was idle, something that wouldn't convey an active pump jack.

The founders of Jonah Bank regard the pump jack as a token of Wyoming's rich and diverse energy industry, as well as their founding of a banking business that is dedicated to the communities it serves.

The plaque reads, "Pump Jack by Joey Bainer. The Jonah Field is our origin story. The oil and gas industry is our foundation. Innovative fuels our growth. May we never stop learning and creating as we continue to Build a Better Wyoming. Proudly celebrating Wyoming's rich energy history and its future. Jonah Bank of Wyoming 2023."

Chief Washakie

Location: Northeast corner of Capitol Avenue and 19th Street
Artist: Guadalupe Barajas
Donor: St. Mark's Episcopal Church

One of the most remarkable figures in Wyoming history is Chief Washakie of the Eastern Shoshones. In his lifetime, he and his people experienced the difficult transition from being free on their own homeland to being included in the United States and later in the State of Wyoming. His life was filled with conflict, and he gained a reputation as a brilliant warrior among both his tribe and their many enemies.

Chief Washakie is remembered as a wise and powerful leader for his people who saw the great changes coming to the land as white settlements moved westward. He was friendly to the white people, and he navigated the bitter struggle between the Indigenous peoples of the Intermountain West and the U.S. government.

Washakie was born between 1804 and 1810, although his exact date of birth is unknown. The Native peoples of the area kept no records, but it is said that he was born in the state now known as Montana to an Umatilla man known as Paseego (Crooked Leg) and a Tussawehee Shoshone woman named Lost Woman. Washakie's first name was Pinah-Quanah, but very little else is known with certainty about his youth.

According to lore, the first major event in his life occurred when warriors from the Black Foot nation attacked a collective camp of Flathead and Lemhi

Shoshone. His father was killed, and Washakie escaped with his mother and siblings. They made their way to another Lemhi village, which took them in. In his early adult years, he left the Lemhi village and at first joined the Bannocks and finally joined the Shoshones around 1830. He had changed his name to Washakie by this time, and his name had several different meanings. The most common is associated with a tale told by interpreter D.B. Huntington in 1840. According to Huntington, when the young man killed his first buffalo, he skinned the buffalo's head, removed all its hair, puckered it up and tied it around a stick with a hole in it so he could blow it up like a bladder. But before he tied the scalp to the stick, he put some stones in it, and when it became perfectly dry, it would rattle. *Washakie* was the Shoshone term for "rattle," and it had been his name ever since.

When Washakie joined the Shoshones, they were a loose grouping of different bands that trained and fought hard against many powerful enemy tribes. Young men were expected to be warriors, and Washakie quickly gained a reputation as being a skilled fighter. Standing at more than six feet tall and powerfully built, Washakie endured many battles, including one in which his left cheek was pierced by a Crow arrow, leaving a permanent scar. His combat prowess and his leadership skills earned him the title of subchief in 1840, and in 1844, he became the head chief of the Shoshones.

Washakie had initiated his association with white people before he joined the Shoshones. He was a skilled hunter and trapper when he met fur traders coming into the western part of Wyoming around 1825. Attracted to the camaraderie and intense atmosphere of the rendezvous, Washakie rarely missed the opportunity to join in between the years 1825 and 1840. It was at these affairs that he likely made his first contact with many well-known fur trappers. He also met men like Father De Smet and missionary Marcus Whitman. Realizing that the whites produced many goods and weapons that his people needed, Washakie encouraged his tribe to trap furs and make robes far beyond their own needs to trade for ammunition, cloth, guns, ornaments and tools.

Washakie also witnessed the growing number of migrants who started crossing his people's land and came to the realization that his small band would be no match for their technology or their numbers. He resolved that he and his people would befriend the whites and work tirelessly to maintain good relations with them.

The friendly demeanor of the Shoshones to the migrants, trappers and other visitors to the area also helped Washakie develop an excellent reputation with people who decided to stay in the region. Mormon leader

Chief Washakie
memorial. *Starley
Talbott photograph.*

Brigham Young met the chief as his people moved into the Salt Lake Valley
and thought highly of him. When the Salt Lake Valley became part of the
United States, Young became governor of Utah territory, and he made
several reports to Washington about the conditions in his jurisdiction and
praised Washakie.

When the United States determined that it needed to create a new treaty
to protect the migrants on the California and Oregon Trails, they called all
the Indigenous peoples in the region to Fort Laramie to discuss what would
become the Fort Laramie Treaty of 1851. Washakie and several of his
tribe attended the historic conference. They were deeply disappointed that
the treaty gave much of their land, including their beloved Wind River
Canyon region, to the Crows—the Shoshones were entirely excluded from
the treaty. Washakie was hurt by this decision, yet he remained determined
to recover his people's lands by other means, and he sought to maintain a

continued friendship with white people. He had no such desire for peace, however, toward his Indigenous enemies, such as the Arapahos, Cheyennes, Crows and Sioux.

By 1866, the Washakie band of the Shoshones and his Bannock allies were suffering from the lack of game in their homeland around the trails. Driven by a need for food, his people turned to their northern territory to hunt. Recently, the Crows had moved into the region and had claimed coveted hunting grounds there for themselves. They, too, had been having difficulty finding food in their own lands and were willing to fight to stay. Washakie's warriors faced off against the Crows in the shadow of a rugged flat-topped bluff in a pitched battle that lasted several days, with Washakie's tribe eventually becoming the victor.

Unfortunately for the Shoshones, this did not end the warfare with their Indigenous neighbors, nor did it resolve the problem of finding food or stopping the incursions of whites into their territory. In 1868, Washakie opened negotiations with the U.S. government to ask for land that would be reserved for the Shoshone people alone. In the Fort Bridger Treaty of 1868, Washakie secured more than 3 million acres of land, including the beloved Wind River Valley, for his people. It was in these lands that the Shoshones could find plenty of food, and they could be close to sacred hot springs that had been cherished by the tribe for many years. Washakie received promises of protection by the U.S. Army in the new reservation. Camp Augur was established at the site of present-day Lander, complemented by a hospital, churches and schools to help teach the Shoshones the ways of their white friends.

However, Washakie was often engaged in constant warfare against the Arapahos, Cheyennes and Sioux. In 1872, he and his warriors repelled a Sioux invasion at Trout Creek, even though they were greatly outnumbered. He faced them again in 1874 in the Battle of Snow Bird, again driving them away from his lands. Unfortunately, his eldest and favorite son was killed in the exchange. According to tribal lore, it was after this tragic loss that Washakie's hair turned pure white. Washakie answered the call to arms by his United States allies in the Great Sioux War of 1876. His warriors lent great service to General Crook at the Battle of the Rosebud against the forces of Crazy Horse and again with General Patrick Connor in driving the Sioux out of the Big Horn Basin.

In his waning years, Washakie's friendship with the white man never dimmed. This friendship was severely challenged at times, yet it endured. The first great challenge came in 1878, when a band of Arapahos was brought to the Wind River Reservation under army escort. Two years prior,

Chief Washakie, ancestral leader of Shoshones. *Starley Talbott photograph.*

the Arapahos had been forced to relocate from the Great Plains to Indian Territory in modern Oklahoma. This band—under the leadership of Sharp Nose, Black Coal, Yellow Calf and Wallowing Bull—had escaped their exile in hopes of returning to their homeland. By the time the army intercepted them in northern Wyoming, winter was approaching, and it was doubtful if the Arapahos would survive a return march. Seeing no alternative, the escorting officers brought the band to Fort Washakie, a newly established post in the Wind River Reservation, to keep them there until they regained their strength and warmer weather returned. The officers at the fort were willing but deferred to Washakie to make the final decision. Washakie had not forgotten that these people had been ruthless enemies only a few years before and was inclined to refuse. But when he saw the nearly starved condition of the women and children, he relented on the promise that the Arapahos would leave as soon as possible. They never did, and Washakie found this fact to be a source of constant irritation for the rest of his life.

However, Washakie maintained his close relationship with government officials and neighbors from surrounding communities, and he continued a growing adherence to Christianity. Washakie had been exposed to this religion in his youth when talking to missionaries he met at the rendezvous. His familiarity with its precepts grew again during his friendship with Brigham Young. It blossomed through his close friendship with Father John Roberts, the Episcopalian minister who had moved to the Wind River Reservation in 1883. Washakie referred to his friend as "white robe," and it was Roberts who finally baptized Washakie into the Episcopal faith in 1898 at the age of ninety-one.

Before this momentous event, Washakie made one last great gift for his white friends. In the Treaty of 1896, Washakie and his chiefs gifted the sacred hot springs near the town of Thermopolis and fifty thousand acres for public use to the State of Wyoming. His only conditions for this gift were that the springs be developed for the free use of the people, regardless of race, color or creed, and that they be overseen by a Shoshone attendant. The State of Wyoming abides by this treaty to this day.

Chief Washakie died on February 20, 1900. Newspapers expressed sorrow at the loss of the chief, and he was hailed as a great warrior and leader and praised for his kindness and wisdom. Washakie was buried after an Episcopalian ceremony attended by more than two thousand people from his tribe and around the state. He was buried with full military honors as a captain in the U.S. Army, the only Indigenous chief to receive such an accolade up to that time. His resting place is marked by a special monument in the cemetery of Fort Washakie, the oldest settlement on the Wind River Reservation. It had originally been named Fort Brown but was renamed in Washakie's honor in 1878.

Chief Washakie remains one of the most exemplary people in Wyoming's history. His friendship helped people find homes throughout the American West. He saved the lives of numerous warriors of his tribe, as well as those within the U.S. Army. Most importantly, his leadership secured an enduring homeland for his nation.

The people of Wyoming held Chief Washakie in such high regard that they placed a sculpture of him in the state capitol, along with his statue in the National Statuary Hall in Washington, D.C. Chief Washakie was recently honored with a sculpture on Capitol Avenue in Cheyenne next to the Episcopal church.

The plaque reads, "Chief Washakie by Guadalupe Barajas. In celebration of the leadership and life of Chief Washakie and his impact on the people of Wyoming. We are especially grateful for his relationship with the Episcopal Church of Wyoming and with the Rev. John Roberts. Donated by the people of St. Mark's Episcopal Church, Cheyenne 2022."

MY RED TRICYCLE

Location: Southeast corner of Capitol Avenue and 19th Street
Artist: Rich Haines
Donors: Dixie and Tom Roberts

Memories of a carefree childhood are depicted in the sculpture *My Red Tricycle*. The young boy, wearing a baseball cap and appearing to observe the

The *My Red Tricycle* statue, honoring children. *Starley Talbott photograph.*

traffic on 19th Street in Cheyenne, looks like he is out for a ride on a sunny day in Wyoming.

This sculpture reminds Don Jones of his young son on his bicycle for the first time, looking daring and full of energy as he zoomed off for his first independent adventure that resulted in an overturned trike. Jones is the stonemason who constructed most of the pedestals for the Capitol Avenue bronze statues and installed most of the sculptures.

For others, the statue might represent the joy and independence of taking a ride on their own tricycle or watching a child or grandchild take those first independent pedals away from mom and dad's watchful eyes.

Donors Dixie and Tom Roberts decided to sponsor the sculpture that was on display at the Deselms Fine Art Gallery in Cheyenne as an early contribution to the bronze project. "It makes you smile every time you pass by the little fellow on the tricycle," said Dixie Roberts.

The Robertses have sponsored three statues along Capitol Avenue, and Dixie serves on the commission for the bronze project. Tom and Dixie have been in attendance at the installations of most of the sculptures along the avenue, helping out in various ways. Dixie is often in charge of placing items in the time capsules imbedded between the stone pedestal and the sculpture.

The plaque reads, "My Red Tricycle by Rich Haines. In Honor of Those Who Teach and Inspire Children to Reach Their Full Potential. Dixie and Tom Roberts 2021."

FAMILY BARBERS LEGACY

Location: Northwest corner of Capitol Avenue and 18th Street
Artist: Guadalupe Barajas
Donors: Jocoby and Gonzales families

The sculpture *Family Barbers Legacy* is dedicated to 150 years of combined service and dedication to their clients and the Cheyenne community by Richard "Dick" Jacoby, Ernie Gonzales and Tom Gonzales.

Richard "Dick" Jacoby attended barber school at the age of twenty-one after completing military service. He operated a business named Dick's Barber Shop for fifty-eight years at the same location in Cheyenne. Dick's business served numerous loyal clients, some of whom spanned five generations.

Ernie Gonzales moved to Cheyenne from New Mexico in 1953 and served in the U.S. Air Force. Following his service, he obtained a degree from a barber college in Denver and began working alongside his brother-in-law, Dick Jacoby, in 1963. Ernie and his wife, Catherine, raised four children and enjoyed family and travel. Ernie was a member of St. Joseph's Catholic Church, American Legion Post 6 and VFW Post 4343. Ernie's life was cut short by cancer, and he died in 2003.

Tom Gonzales attended Colorado Barber School in Denver and became the first barber to work at the Officer's Club at Warren Air Force Base. He later opened his own business, Lincolnway Barber Shop. Tom was known for his skills as a barber and his ability to connect with his clients. He was often included in family photos celebrating a child's first haircut, and his shop was known as a gathering place where folks could share stories, jokes and news of the day. Tom's legacy lives on in the bronze statue created in his honor, which features his grandson Tommy sitting in the barber chair.

Left: *Family Barbers Legacy*. *Starley Talbott photograph*.

Below: Don Jones, stonemason, bringing the *Family Barbers* statue to its place on Capitol Avenue. *Starley Talbott photograph*.

The plaque reads, "Legacy by Guadalupe Barajas. In commemoration of Richard 'Dick' Jacoby, Ernie Gonzales and Tom Gonzales for 150 years of combined service and dedication to their clients and the Cheyenne community. Donated by the Jacoby and Gonzales families 2023."

VICE ADMIRAL FRANCIS MCINERNEY

Location: Southwest corner of Capitol Avenue and 18th Street
Artist: Joel Turner
Donors: Diane and Daniel E. White, Catherine and Edward F. Murray III,
John T. McInerney and Sara Murphy

When the graduating class of 1916 walked across the stage to receive their diplomas, they were facing a world that had broken apart. The terror of World War I had broken out only a few years before. The United States, safely protected by the vast expanse of the Atlantic Ocean, seemed to escape from the cataclysm, for a time. However, President Woodrow Wilson asked Congress to declare war on Germany and its allies in April 1917. The people of the United States were now involved in the greatest war in human history, and its youth faced a reckoning.

Francis Xavier McInerney answered his nation's call. Born in Cheyenne to Phyllis and Thomas McInerney in 1899, Francis had already graduated from high school and had spent one year at the University of Colorado before America was plunged into war. Francis joined the U.S. Navy, a move that would shape the course of his life and win him great renown.

On June 13, 1917, McInerney entered the U.S. Naval Academy in Annapolis, Maryland. He quickly adapted to the rigorous course of study and involved himself in sports, playing on the baseball and basketball squads. In the summer of 1918, he served his midshipman cruise aboard the old battleship USS *Ohio*. The Great War ended before he was able to finish his course of study, yet his devotion to duty remained. He served his second training cruise on a series of battleships: the USS *Mississippi*, the USS *Texas*, the USS *Utah* and the USS *Florida*. McInerney graduated with a commission as an ensign. He had gained quite a reputation among his classmates by this time. In the *Lucky Bag* yearbook, the editorial staff commented:

Someone once said of Mac that he was as steady as a church-spire, but this is not correct; church-spires have been known to blow down or topple over, or otherwise deport themselves in un-church-spire-like manner, but not so Mac. He's just as study and levelheaded as the day is long, and when you add to this an inexpressible fund of wholesome good humor and incurable optimism you have a thumbnail sketch of one of "21"'s most likeable personalities.

After graduation, McInerney was immediately assigned to the powerful USS *New Mexico*, flagship of the U.S. Pacific Fleet, where he served for one year.

From the start, it seemed that McInerney would serve his naval career on the mighty battleships, but this was not to be. After only one year aboard the *New Mexico*, McInerney was drawn to service on an entirely different class of ship, the destroyer. Smaller than the powerful castles of steel on which he had served before, destroyers were a class of ship built for duty on patrol, hunting submarines or escorting larger ships. While heavily armed, these small vessels relied more on speed and maneuverability for survival rather than the heavy armor that protected the battleships. McInerney enjoyed serving on destroyers, and from 1921 to 1927, he served on a variety of these vessels on both coasts. It was while serving on one of these ships that he married Katherine Hammann of Torrington, Connecticut, in 1924, and the couple became the parents of two children, Joan and Robert.

In 1927, McInerney was stationed at the Naval Torpedo Station at Newport, Rhode Island. From there he made frequent cruises on the USS *Dobin*, a tender ship to service destroyers at sea, until he accepted an assignment to the Judge Advocate General's Office for the Navy in Washington, D.C., in 1932. Once in the nation's capital, he attended George Washington University Law School, receiving his Bachelor of Law degree in 1935. McInerney assumed the practice of law in the District Court and U.S. Court of Appeals for the District of Columbia yet returned to sea aboard the USS *Concord*, a light cruiser, in the Pacific until 1938. On July 15, 1938, he returned to Annapolis, this time as an instructor at the Postgraduate School at the Naval Academy until May 29, 1940. On June 22 of that year, he assumed command of the USS *Smith*, a destroyer.

By that time, the world was again embroiled in war. Germany had once again launched a devastating war of aggression in Europe and this time was joined by the powerful forces of Imperial Japan. Like the First World War, America was again neutral, but it was already gearing up for war. McInerney and the USS *Smith* were operating out of San Francisco on December 7, 1941, when the Japanese navy launched its infamous surprise attack on Pearl Harbor. The *Smith* became part of Destroyer Squadron 5, responsible for escorting ships from the West Coast to Pearl Harbor and back. On February 1, 1942, McInerney and his ship were attached to the Australian and New Zealand Army (ANZAC), where he became senior commander of American destroyers operating with their Australian and New Zealand counterparts in the South Pacific. From March 24 to August 2, McInerney commanded Destroyer Squadron 9 during the Battle of the Coral Sea and early fighting in the Solomon Islands. Afterward, he temporarily took command of Destroyer Squadron 2 while recovering from battle before assuming command of Destroyer Squadron 21 on March 10, 1943, where he took command of another destroyer, the USS *Nicholas*.

Upon taking command of the USS *Nicholas*, McInerney was returning to the American campaign to secure the Solomon Islands. This archipelago contained hundreds of islands, many of which were fortified by the Japanese before the war, including Guadalcanal, on which America launched its Pacific counteroffensive in 1942. The many hundreds of islands and their shallow surrounding waters proved to be very dangerous for the navy, not only because much of the seaway was uncharted but also because the Japanese navy undertook a massive campaign to reinforce their island bastions during the American invasion. Multiple battles, often at night, were fought and proved to be some of the toughest fighting for the navy during the war.

On July 5, 1943, McInerney and his destroyers were attached to a task force under the command of Admiral Walden L. Ainsworth, charged with landing marines on the island of Kolombangara. While the main fleet covered the invasion, McInerney maneuvered his squadron through the tight confines between islands while exchanging gunfire with Japanese defenders on Kolombangara, Vila and Bairoko Harbor. Just before midnight on July 6, seven Japanese destroyers under the command of Rear Admiral Akiyama Teruo attacked the task force. The fierce nighttime engagement was a hard-won victory for the Americans and came with heavy losses. Just before dawn, Japanese destroyers *Suzukaze* and *Tanikaze* launched a torpedo attack on the USS *Helena*, a light cruiser, which was struck by three torpedoes. The terrific detonations ripped the American ship into three pieces killing 168 crew before going down, with the remaining survivors spilling into the sea. Alerted to the calamity, McInerney ordered his destroyer, the USS *Nicholas*, and the USS *Radford* to race to the scene and rescue everyone they could. During the effort, McInerney's ships were attacked by the destroyers *Amagiri*

Vice Admiral Francis
Xavier McInerney
memorial. *Starley Talbott
photograph.*

and *Hasuyuki* on three separate occasions. Evading torpedoes and gunfire, McInerney's ships drove off the enemy vessels while refusing to abandon the stricken sailors. Because of his crew's actions, McInerney was able to save more than 700 men that night. After the battle, the remaining American ships, all with various degrees of damage, retreated from the area. During what became known as the Battle of Kula Gulf, the ships McInerney served with destroyed or drove off ten enemy ships.

Only one week later, it was reported that there were still survivors of the USS *Helena* awaiting rescue. These sailors had swum to shore on the enemy-occupied island of Vella Levalla and were in great danger of capture. On the evening of July 15, McInerney led his destroyer squadron into the battle zone again under the cover of darkness through the dangerous waters known as "the Slot" toward the island. While the rest of his fleet conducted the rescue operation, McInerney ordered the USS *Nicholas* to engage with enemy forces

A plaque on the pedestal of the McInerney sculpture. *Starley Talbott photograph.*

on Vella Levalla and the nearby New Georgia Island. Engaging again with shore artillery and attacks by enemy aircraft, the USS *Nicholas* served as the perfect diversion to keep the Japanese occupied while the task force rescued 165 additional sailors. Both the task force and the USS *Nicholas* retreated back through the Slot the next day with no damage to any of the ships involved. Because of his actions during these two engagements, McInerney earned the Navy Cross, the Silver Star and ultimately the Legion of Merit for the daring rescue raid.

In August 1943, McInerney was promoted to represent the Commander of Destroyers in the South Pacific, and in March 1944, he became chief of staff for the Commander Operation Training Command of the Pacific Fleet. On June 5, 1945, he assumed command of the battleship USS *Washington* after it and its crew had completed a long string of combat operations. He commanded it on its return to the West Coast, making stops at Guam and Pearl Harbor before reaching Puget Sound Navy Yard on June 23. The USS *Washington* was in refit when the atomic bombs were dropped on Hiroshima and Nagasaki and through the Japanese surrender on September 2, 1945.

After the refit of the USS *Washington* was completed, McInerney was stationed at the Naval Receiving Station at San Francisco from October 1946 to January 1948. He then assumed command of the Pacific Light Cruiser Division through January 1950. He then led the Pacific Amphibious Training Command through October 1951 and then commanded Amphibious Group III from October 1951 to March 1953. Thereafter he was the senior member of the Board of Inspection and Survey through October of 1954 and then president of the General Courts-Martial of the Eleventh Naval District until June 1955. McInerney retired from the navy as a vice-admiral on June 30, 1955, and died on June 24, 1956, in San Francisco.

At his eulogy, the U.S. Navy made a statement about this remarkable officer that summed up his stellar career:

Vice Admiral McInerney will be remembered by the naval service as one of our most courageous leaders. During his remarkable career, he was awarded numerous citations for outstanding performances of duty during operations against the enemy in World War II, and the Korean Conflict. It is men such as he who, by leadership and devotion to duty, provide a reservoir of inspiration and strength for those who follow.

The USS *McInerney*, a Perry Class frigate named in his honor, was launched on November 4, 1978, with the motto "Fast, Fearless, Gallant." The ship was decommissioned on August 31, 2010, and currently serves with the Pakistani navy as the *Alamgir*.

MY LITTLE DEER

Location: Northeast corner of Capitol Avenue and 18ᵗʰ Street
Artist: Christine Knapp
Donors: Bill and Beth Edwards

The sculpture *My Little Deer* spoke to the love of Cheyenne and Wyoming for Bill and Beth Edwards when they attended a reception featuring the Capitol Avenue Bronze Project in 2021. The couple were inspired by the legacy project and decided that it would be a fitting tribute for their family, including their grandchildren, who represent the sixth generation of the family in Wyoming.

The *My Little Deer* sculpture. *Starley Talbott photograph.*

The lifelike statue of the mule deer, a doe nuzzling her fawn, was captured by the artist, Christine Knapp. Mule deer are found in varied locations throughout Wyoming, including on ranch and farmland throughout the state.

Beth Edwards chose the sculpture, which reminded her of the many happy times spent riding along with her grandfather Chris Bourne and her mother, Barbara Murray. Often, when they drove on roads traversing the high plains around Cheyenne, they were thrilled to see wild animals like deer and antelope. "My grandfather and mother would often burst into song when they saw the deer and antelope playing, including the chorus of 'Home on the Range,'" Beth said. Those happy days now become a legacy for the Edwards with the installation of the statue on Capitol Avenue.

Beth Murray and Bill Edwards met in history class at Cheyenne Central High School. The class was taught by the late William "Bill" Dubois III, a beloved community member, who sang at the couple's wedding in 1977. They have three children and seven grandchildren.

Both Bill and Beth are active in business and volunteer activities in Cheyenne. Bill operated Edwards Construction Company for many years.

Beth's love of Cheyenne and Wyoming became the foundation for her many volunteer positions. She has a special interest in the Old West Museum that began when, as Beth Murray, she served as Miss Frontier for Cheyenne Frontier Days™ in 1974. A few years later, she helped to organize the Dazee Bristol Society and the Carriage Ball, both former events during the annual frontier celebration. She was the chairperson for the Breast Cancer Pink Day at CFD from 2002 to 2015. She was also a member of the Wheels, a group of women who assist in the care of costumes and carriages at the Old West Museum.

Other community organizations including the Boys & Girls Club, Comea Shelter, Animal Shelter, Civic League and the 150th Anniversary Celebration of Cheyenne benefited from the volunteer efforts of the Edwards and many other Cheyenne citizens.

When the *My Little Deer* sculpture was installed on Capitol Avenue, Bill and Beth Edwards and family were present. Beth Edwards concluded by saying, "It is our hope that future generations of our family will become part of this legacy project in Cheyenne."

The plaque reads, "My Little Deer by Christine Knapp. 'Home, home on the range, where the deer and the antelope play.' Dedicated to our children, grandchildren, and all the future generations of Cheyenne. Bill and Beth Edwards 2022."

Devoted

Location: Southeast corner of Capitol Avenue and 18th Street
Artist: Chuck Weaver
Donors: Multiple

Chuck Weaver was asked to create *Devoted* for the Capitol Bronze project; it was an opportunity to do something for the community where he grew up. After graduating from high school in Cheyenne, he joined the navy and later worked on missiles. He had dabbled in art previously, being primarily interested in creating designs and pinstriping on his friend's cars. It wasn't until he was living with his family in Denver as a pipefitter that he truly began pursuing his art career. After taking a weekend oil painting class, he was inspired to do more. Utilizing funds from GI educational assistance, he enrolled at Colorado State University and relocated to Fort Collins to study art. After learning all that he could about three-dimensional art, he began work at a bronze foundry to refine his skills there.

His subject, the wolf, has been part of the human imagination for uncounted generations. Found in Europe, Asia and North America, the wolf is a universally recognized predator that has developed both good and bad cultural connotations. The largest of canines, the wolf is renowned for its adaptability, high speed, keen senses and persistence in the hunt. Its most formidable characteristic is that the wolf rarely hunts alone, especially in winter. Relying on others of its kind, the wolf is a potent carnivore relying on packs, sometimes twenty-four strong, to pursue and bring down prey much larger than themselves. Beyond the mutual benefit of hunting together, the pack is a family consisting of an adult breeding pair, along with their offspring. The members of the pack are highly social and form strong bonds with one another. These bonds help in the procurement of food, the care for the young and defense against intruders from other packs. Within this social organization, wolves have developed a very complex method of communication that is visual, tactile, auditory and even chemical.

These characteristics have intrigued humans across the world. Some find the behavior of the wolf to be similar to that of people and have woven stories and legends of the wolf into their cultures as a positive force. Others find menace in this highly intelligent and efficient carnivore and have sought to control or even eradicate it. How this relationship developed through time was often determined by the societal relationship between people and their natural environment. If the environment is perceived as something to be conserved, protected or integral to a culture, then the wolf may be seen as a kindred spirit, an animal worthy of protection or even as a hero. Conversely, if a society is intent on transforming the environment into an area to be used by humans for their benefit, the wolf may become an invader, a ruthless and cruel adversary, even a villain.

The gray wolf is a controversial animal in Wyoming. While attitudes in greater American society up to the 1900s were negative against the wolf, Native Americans often depicted the wolf differently. The Shoshone people, for instance, revered the wolf as the creator god who consistently had to help his brother, Coyote, get out of trouble. For the homesteaders and ranchers who started coming to Wyoming in the middle of the nineteenth century,

The *Devoted* sculpture.
Starley Talbott photograph.

however, the wolf was an obstacle to success. It was a pragmatic matter to remove the threat of the wolf so that livestock could thrive and a livelihood could be carved out of Wyoming's difficult environment. By the 1900s, the wolf had been eradicated from its habitat in our state.

Through the course of the twentieth and early twenty-first centuries, however, strong support for maintaining and reestablishing nature's balance became prevalent in the attitudes of people living in growing urban communities across the nation who relied less on nature's bounty as a means of survival and instead appreciated it for its wildness, beauty and recreational opportunities. Environmental groups sought to reintroduce the wolf to regenerate the nation's natural ecosystems, and the U.S. government reintroduced forty-one wolves to Yellowstone National Park beginning in 1995. The animals have been successful in repopulating their numbers to the point that the government removed their endangered species designation in 2012. Ranchers and farmers in the state continue to express alarm at the presence of these predators, and acceding to the need to prevent wolves from becoming an economic problem, the Wyoming Game and Fish Department has implemented a management plan for their control.

Chuck Weaver was aware of these controversies when he created *Devoted*. Instead of focusing on the controversy of the wolf, he decided to depict one of the noble characteristics of the predator. "About the time I did this sculpture, there was a lot of discussion regarding the re-introduction of wolves, about their being endangered or not, their impact on the area, etc. Reading about the species, I learned they are considered monogamous, dedicated to one mate. I chose to depict this pair expressing that bond."

Chuck Weaver died before his sculpture *Devoted* was dedicated.

Working Together for Others

Location: Northwest corner of 17th Street and Capitol Avenue
Artist: Joel Turner
Donors: Larry and Connie Atwell

The bronze sculpture *Working Together for Others* is dedicated to those Cheyenne citizens—past, current and future—who have recognized that by working together with those from different backgrounds, they are successfully building a greater community for all.

Larry and Connie Atwell, donors of the sculpture, represent the ultimate concept behind the statue, featuring a handshake between cooperating people who work together to make their community a welcome place for all the people who live there.

The Atwells moved to Cheyenne from Cincinnati in 1973 when they became the owners of Wilson Equipment and Supply Company. They operated the company until 1986.

Along with operating a company in Cheyenne, both Larry and Connie are active members and volunteers in many organizations in the city and the state. Connie served on the state board for Girl Scouts, worked with local Girl Scouts and Boy Scouts, served on volunteer committees for Saint

The *Working Together for Others* sculpture. *Starley Talbott photograph.*

Mary's Bishop Guild and Cathedral Guild and has been an active member of Cheyenne Civic League for forty-nine years.

Larry Atwell served on the Greater Cheyenne Chamber of Commerce Board of Directors and was chairman of the board in 1984. He was hired as the chamber director in 1988, serving in this position for nineteen years.

Of his service as chamber director, Atwell said, "It always impressed me how in Cheyenne, on a number of occasions, various people had worked together to achieve what I had considered significant progress."

During the nineteen years that Atwell served as the director, he said it was like taking one big roller coaster ride. He said that he was never able to just sit back and enjoy the ride because there were always challenges to meet. However, by working together, many people helped these challenges be met.

"I have always felt this type of effort needed to be recognized and encouraged and had told my wife and children that I wanted my estate to sponsor such outdoor art to accomplish that goal," Larry said. The Atwells have assisted in small ways the efforts of many individuals in promoting public art in Cheyenne. They saw the opportunity to sponsor a sculpture for the Capitol Avenue Bronze Project as a way to reach the goal of recognition for the community's accomplishments.

The Atwells worked with sculpture artist Joel Turner to turn their concept of "working together" into a sculpture for Capitol Avenue. The bronze depicts two people, who may be of different race or gender and come from different walks of life, shaking hands and agreeing to work together.

As each of the bronze sculptures was installed along Capitol Avenue, a time capsule was placed between the statue and the stone pedestal. Many people have placed small items in the capsules, and the donors have often placed items important to them or write notes for future generations to read. Larry Atwell wrote these words for the *Working Together for Others* time capsule: "When this time capsule is opened, we hope you have found information about Cheyenne from years past and information about the activities and interests of the people who were interested enough to install this bronze. It is hoped you will be able to find some of our descendants so they may see how much we enjoyed and appreciated Cheyenne. We hope that the citizens of Cheyenne were inspired by the bronze 'Working Together' and have continued that effort with Cheyenne becoming a vital, enjoyable and great community in which to live."

The plaque reads, "Working Together for Others by Joel Turner. Dedicated to those Cheyenne citizens, past, current, and future who have recognized that by Working Together with those from different backgrounds, they are successfully building a greater community for all. Donated by the Larry & Connie Atwell Family 2023."

Earning His Oats

Location: Southwest corner of Capitol Avenue and 17th Street
Artist: Del Pettigrew
Donor: Tara Nethercott

The sculpture *Earning His Oats* depicts a draft horse in harness pulling a load up an incline. The statue represents draft horses, which are large and powerful animals well suited for hauling heavy loads and plowing fields.

Sculptor Del Pettigrew had no formal training as a sculpture artist, but he knew horses, said his wife, Martha Pettigrew. Del created the statue of a draft horse pulling a load as a symbol of persistence and tenacity when

The *Earning His Oats* sculpture. *Starley Talbott photograph.*

performing any type of work. Del Pettigrew died in 2017 and "left a legacy in art of the animals he created," said Martha.

Donor Tara Nethercott is a Cheyenne attorney and a Wyoming state senator from Laramie County. Nethercott said that the statue of the horse climbing uphill is a reminder of the persistence and tenacity required in the practice of the law and as a representative in the legislature.

The plaque reads, "Earning His Oats by Del Pettigrew. In honor of the strength, grace and fortitude of Jim & Judy Nethercott. Donated by Tara Nethercott 2022."

NORMA'S CALF

Location: Northeast corner of Capitol Avenue and 17th Street
Artist: Rich Haines
Donor: Harvey Deselms

The sculpture of a baby calf sitting atop a stone pedestal on Capitol Avenue and 17th Street has special meaning for the donor, Harvey Deselms.

Deselms grew up on the family ranch near Albin, Wyoming. His parents, Kenneth and Norma Deselms, inspired their children to value and respect

The *Norma's Calf* sculpture, honoring agriculture. *Starley Talbott photograph.*

their agricultural heritage. They also heaped love and care on their children along with the livestock on the ranch.

When Harvey established his art gallery in Cheyenne, one of his employees was a high school student named Rich Haines. Rich became interested in sculpture art and photography when he took a class in high school and when he worked at the Deselms Fine Art Gallery.

Haines's interest in photography led to him traveling to the Deselms ranch in eastern Laramie County. Norma Deselms took Rich out to the pasture to take photos of the calves. The last photo of the day was of a "bucket calf." The animal was Norma's favorite because she fed it with a bucket of milk every day, as the mother cow was unable to provide milk for the calf.

A few years later, when Haines completed the sculpture of the baby calf, he named it *Norma's Calf* in honor of Norma Deselms. The Deselms family thought it was an appropriate way to honor their parents and their agricultural heritage.

The plaque reads, "Norma's Calf by Rich Haines. Gifted to Cheyenne in memory of Kenneth S. Deselms and Norma J. Sandberg Deselms by their children: Howard, Bob, Shirley, Joe and Harvey 2021."

MITTENS

Location: Southeast corner of Capitol Avenue and 17ᵗʰ Street
Artist: Chris Navarro
Donors: Susan and Doug Samuelson

Mittens is a fitting name for the sculpture honoring one of Wyoming's oldest historic ranches, Warren Livestock Company, founded in 1883. Francis E. Warren, later elected as Wyoming's territorial governor and the first state governor and then as a United States senator, established the ranch northeast of Cheyenne.

Warren stocked the ranch with both cattle and sheep, as did many early cattle barons. In 1898, there were 1,940,021 sheep and 706,000 cattle recorded in Wyoming. Francis Warren served as the president of the National Wool Growers Association from 1901 to 1907. Therefore, the statue of a sheep named Mittens is a proper tribute to the Warren Livestock Company.

The current owners of Warren Livestock, Susan and Doug Samuelson, operate the ranch much the same as the Warren family did. Technology has been adapted to make the ranch run more efficiently, while both cattle and sheep continue to occupy the land. The Samuelsons are the third owners of historic Warren Livestock, following the Warren family and the Etchepare family.

During the years when the ranch was operated by the Warren family, F.E. Warren's son, Frederick (Fred) incorporated innovative management techniques. Fred worked with Dr. John Hill of the University of Wyoming to create a specialized breed of sheep named Warhill that is still raised on the ranch today.

Susan Samuelson, vice-president of Warren Livestock, has earned the title of "Head Bo Peep" because she is involved with the sheep, especially during lambing and shearing season. Susan assists the Peruvian sheepherders in the spring when the lambs are born in the pasture. She explained how the newborn lambs and mothers are brought to the sheep shed "hospital" in the "Lambulance," a camper-like facility on the back of a pickup. "Several ewes and lambs can be loaded and brought to the shed where they are placed in small enclosures called 'jugs' until they are several weeks old," she said. The ranch includes around five bands of sheep, each band being assigned to a sheepherder from Peru. The herders usually are allowed to remain for three years in the United States until they return to Peru. The herders no longer live in sheep wagons, as in the past, but in modern campers. In addition,

The *Mittens* sculpture, honoring a historic ranch. *Starley Talbott photograph.*

Colorado State University veterinary students complete a senior seminar at Warren Livestock for six weeks in April and May.

Following lambing season, the sheep are sheared in the historical shearing shed at Warren Livestock by shearers from Chile. Susan Samuelson often helps during the shearing operation by doctoring minor wounds and helping cook for the workers.

Long before Susan became "Head Bo Peep" at Warren Livestock, she was a teacher at several schools in Cheyenne. She grew up in Casper in the McMurry family, graduated from the University of Wyoming and served as a vocational reading specialist for twenty-three years. She married Doug Samuelson in 1984.

Doug Samuelson, president of Warren Livestock, grew up in Riverton, Wyoming. He earned a degree in wildlife biology and worked on the family ranch in Riverton for several years. He also served as a habitat biologist for the Wyoming Game and Fish Commission.

Doug and Susan Samuelson lived for sixteen years at the Wyoming Hereford Ranch near Cheyenne, before purchasing Warren Livestock in 2000. They are the parents of one daughter and grandparents of one granddaughter.

The Samuelsons became interested in the Capitol Avenue Bronze Project when they saw Chris Navarro's sculpture of a lamb at the Cheyenne Frontier Days™ art show. They chose to purchase the sculpture and donate *Mittens* to highlight the fact that Warren Livestock, true to its heritage, continues to produce lambs, just as the ranch did when the Warrens were the owners. Susan serves as a member of the Capitol Avenue Bronze Commission. She is also a volunteer for the Wyoming Community Foundation and Jennie Gordon's Hunger Initiative, sponsored by Wyoming's first lady.

A large portion of Warren Livestock has been donated to a conservation easement with the Wyoming Stock Growers Land Trust. As stewards of the land, the Samuelsons honor the history of Warren Livestock by maintaining the tradition of grazing cattle and sheep, while also preserving and improving the landscape and wildlife habitat.

The plaque reads, "Mittens by Chris Navarro. In honor of Warren Livestock, its founder and all the men and women who have worked the land since 1883, this statue is dedicated. Doug & Susan Samuelson 7XL 2021."

Rarin' to Ride

Location: Northeast corner of Capitol Avenue and 16th Street
Artist: George Lundeen
Donor: Wyoming Bank and Trust

The sense of anticipation is electric when one stands next to *Rarin' to Ride*. A young boy eagerly embraces a saddle, ready to have his turn. He wants to participate—he wants to be part of something wonderful. He is eager for the challenge and to be part of our western experience. From head to toe, he is dressed in iconic clothing—hat, boots, chaps and gloves. He wants to be a cowboy.

Children have always looked up to heroes and have been inspired to emulate them. They want to be astronauts, firemen, policemen, soldiers, doctors, ballerinas—the list is infinite. Who is this "cowboy," and what makes him someone who will light up the eyes of boys and girls and still

The *Rarin' to Ride* sculpture. *Starley Talbott photograph.*

ensnare the imagination of adults across the world, even though it seems that his time is long gone?

Historically, the role of the cowboy is ancient. The need to have people to manage domesticated livestock began when the first herds of domesticated cattle appeared nearly eleven thousand years ago in Southwest Asia. The practice of raising these animals gradually spread to other areas. By the discovery of the New World in 1492, the Portuguese and Spaniards had been associated with cattle for millennia, and it was natural that they would bring this favorite food source with them.

The Spaniards brought cattle and horses to the Americas and established ranches in 1519. As the Spanish empire grew, the range of the cattle ranches and those who worked them expanded. By the 1700s, Spanish ranches were operating in the southwestern part of the modern United States and as far south as Argentina. Indigenous people were taught Spanish techniques for raising and caring for cattle. These people, known as *vaqueros*, were renowned for their skills in horsemanship and roping techniques. They were a vital component of this purely Hispanic enterprise before the first Americans came into their lands to trade in the 1820s. After the discovery of gold in California in 1849, Americans from the East flooded into the former territories of Mexico, and the Hispanic techniques for raising livestock spread up the West Coast into Oregon, north into modern Idaho and west to the Hawaiian Islands. Hawaiian cowboys, known as *paniolos*, were on the islands as early as 1823. As cattle drives began to take longhorn cattle from the wilds of Texas after the American Civil War to feed the growing cities of America's East, the men who drove them borrowed the techniques, dress, tools and even some of the language from the *vaqueros*. They became the prototypical cowboys that have dominated western lore ever since.

The first cattle driven to Wyoming by Texas cowboys came in the mid-1860s as part of government contracts to help feed Indigenous tribes in the Intermountain West. This became increasingly important as the buffalo herds that were a staple part of the Native diet were slowly disappearing from their traditional ranges. Treaties to uphold peace were created with many Indigenous peoples in the area, and part of the deal was the importation of Texas cattle. The U.S. Army also needed cattle to feed its soldiers at the far-flung outposts across the landscape. Miners, too, especially in Colorado and Montana, relied on cattle drives to feed them as they scoured the landscape for riches. John W. Iliff brought thousands of cattle to feed the track-laying crews of the Union Pacific Railroad along with the citizens of the new town of Cheyenne and Fort D.A. Russell.

The newcomers quickly realized the benefit of Wyoming's wide-open rangeland, with its mild climate and nutritious grasses. Within a few years, the cattle industry had become the most profitable in the territory and made many ranchers and their investors fantastically wealthy. Powerful associations emerged to guide the new trade, but it still took men to look after the animals and round them up for the spring branding and the fall cattle drives. The Wyoming cattle industry experienced booms and busts, but the cowboy remained. Riding for the brand, men ranging in age from teenagers to wizened codgers in their seventies endured hardships, injuries and low pay in exchange for a life of freedom and hard work. They came from all walks of life seeking a variety of things: adventure, solitude and, perhaps, an escape from their past. Regardless of circumstances or consequences, the cowboy lifestyle appealed to many. The demands of the job were harsh and often changed them as they adapted to their new environments out of necessity, often acquiring estimable qualities.

The cowboy epitomizes a perceived concept about the frontier, projected onto it by people from outside. For many people who occupied the settled lands of the East, the West was a fearsome and mysterious place. Filled with great dangers, it was also a place of outstanding opportunities. It took bold people, like cowboys, to head out into the land and live their lives there.

Western characters depicted in novels held a fascination for people in the East. Trapped in their familiar and mundane surroundings on farms and in factories, the sense of adventure that lay beyond the western horizon had great appeal. None was better at capturing this sense of adventure and fascination than Buffalo Bill Cody. A real-life rider of the Pony Express, a buffalo hunter and army scout, Cody was also an itinerate showman who brought a taste of the authentic West around the world beginning in the 1880s. The heroes of the real West were tangible and touchable, and the excitement of the gunfight and the cattle drive was palpable. With the closing of the American frontier by the Census Bureau in 1890, people's interest in what was soon to become a bygone way of life intensified.

In 1897, a new phenomenon was born in Cheyenne. Seeking to capture the public's fascination with the West, promoters from the Union Pacific Railroad and businessmen from the community joined forces to create a celebration of Cheyenne's storied past and the cattle industry on which it was built. Combined with a nascent form of rodeo, a sporting event highlighting the skills of legendary cowboys against the power of untamed horses and cattle, the founders of Cheyenne Frontier Days™ created a new form of festival that combined true cowboy sports with the participation of authentic contributors to America's past, including soldiers and Indigenous peoples. Here was an event where people could come into the West to see and interact with the people who lived there. It was wildly popular, and the cowboy's legendary status grew.

Part of the appeal of the cowboy was that he was the hero of the common man. In the Gilded Age, he represented a character of quality in the class struggle between the haves and the have-nots. He was generally depicted as not being well spoken and out of place anywhere but in the West, yet he also exuded courage, self-reliance and valor.

Owen Wister's novel *The Virginian*, published in 1902, sealed the cowboy's destiny of becoming a cultural hero. Set in Wyoming and inspired by the Johnson County War, the novel brought to the masses the quintessential tale of a rugged, silent and independent cowboy standing up for the innocent and for what was right in the face of evil. Early movie companies seized on Wister's formula and created hundreds of films featuring real cowboy actors and stuntmen, some taken right from the open range of Wyoming. Even though the early movies were silent, the films dazzled their spectators. Building on the tradition of the nineteenth-century dime novels, the stories continued to enthrall their audiences.

By the 1920s, the cowboy had become a mythic hero. He had become a complex character. According to Robert Hine, author of *The American West: An Interpretive History*, the cowboy "was at once regional and universal, violent and gentle, boastful and modest, lawless and honorable, competitive and compassionate, savage and civilized."

It was during this time that the cowboy became something of a savior for the people of Wyoming. Struck by dire economic times and desperate to find any means of bringing money into their communities, citizens across the state began to offer authentic western experiences to the multitudes of visitors seeking recreational wonders that Wyoming offered. Wyoming became the home for numerous dude ranches, rodeos and festivals. People from urban settings who had never set foot on a ranch or gotten on a horse began donning cowboy hats and boots to reflect what the public had seen in the movies or visualized in their novels. It may not have been an authentic vision of the true Wyoming experience, but it worked and remains an important part of Wyoming's tourism industry.

Perhaps this is the cowboy the boy depicted in *Rarin' to Ride* wants to emulate. This young man is inspired by the cowboy lifestyle that is still a deep part of what makes Wyoming the wonderful place it is. The young man is surrounded by the cowboy image wherever he looks. It is on the license plates, hats, T-shirts, jackets, bumper stickers, advertisements and buildings. It is manifested by the cowboys and cowgirls who are incredible athletes participating in the glory of rodeo sports throughout the land. Most importantly, it is reflected in his friends and family who have adopted the cowboy lifestyle as their own. And they, of course, are the greatest heroes of all.

Rarin' to Ride was donated by the Wyoming Bank and Trust. The Federal Land and Security Company arrived in Wyoming to advance investors' interest in new migration to southeast Wyoming around 1900. Many of the new settlers came to practice dry farming, a technique that held great promise to allow profitable crops to grow without substantial irrigation. The company established a new base of operations in a town it created called Luther and established the Luther State Bank in 1907, specifically to meet the needs of the farmers and residents in the area. The town was later renamed Burns after a local Union Pacific Railroad worker who was killed in 1910, near the same time the community established its first post office.

On May 5, 1919, thirty-two stockholders launched the Farmers State Bank of Burns. The bank eventually absorbed the original Luther State Bank in 1928 and thrived, even though Wyoming was in the throes of an economic depression that had spelled the end of many similar institutions. Dennis Wallace purchased the bank in 1970, moved its headquarters to Cheyenne in 1995 and changed the name to the Wyoming Bank & Trust. The Wallace family became supporters of numerous community projects along with a great interest in public art. They had met and befriended Colorado artist George Lundeen before the Capitol Avenue Bronze Project was launched. When Jeff Wallace, Dennis's son, became a member of the project commission, George Lundeen was chosen to create a sculpture that the family thought captured the essence of Cheyenne and its people. This young cowboy, eagerly awaiting his turn to saddle a horse and ride, captures the spirit the Wallace family celebrates about the citizens of Wyoming.

The plaque reads, "Rarin' to Ride by George Lundeen. In honor of the people of Wyoming and their pioneering spirit for more than a century. The Wallace Family/Wyoming Bank and Trust 2022."

DAKOTA WIND

Location: Northwest corner of Capitol Avenue and 16th Street
Artist: Martha Pettigrew
Donors: Phyllis and Jim O'Connor

The sculpture of *Dakota Wind* depicts a Native woman wrapped in a buffalo robe, huddled against the rigors of the wind and cold. The statue on Cheyenne's Capitol Avenue is a scale model of a larger sculpture by artist Martha Pettigrew that is displayed in Sioux Falls, South Dakota.

Phyllis and Jim O'Connor are the donors of *Dakota Wind* and offered this sculpture as a way to "[r]espect and honor all the different people of Wyoming." When the O'Connors were deciding on a sculpture to add to the Capitol Avenue bronze collection, they chose one that represented the impacts that Natives and women have made on the state of Wyoming.

The *Dakota Wind* sculpture, honoring a Native woman. *Starley Talbott photograph.*

Jim O'Connor grew up on a ranch in South Dakota located near several Native reservations. He graduated from South Dakota State University, where he met his future wife, Phyllis. The couple moved to Cheyenne in 1977 with the idea that they might live there temporarily. Jim worked for the Wyoming Department of Transportation, and Phyllis was a registered nurse. They grew to enjoy Cheyenne and the people, never leaving the magic city of the plains.

Since retirement after thirty-one years at WYDOT for Jim and thirty-two years of nursing at Cheyenne Regional Medical Center for Phyllis, the couple have been involved with many activities in Cheyenne. Phyllis serves on the board of directors for Health Works, is a member of PEO and First

Presbyterian Church and is an avid quilter. Jim is a member of Kiwanis Club and Holy Trinity Catholic Church. He also serves as a driver for Meals on Wheels and volunteers at Friday Food Bag.

As avid fans of art appreciation and the leadership of Harvey Deselms, Jim and Phyllis wanted to show residents and visitors their pride of living in Cheyenne and to share the historic heritage of the city and state. They met with Deselms and artist Martha Pettigrew to choose the sculpture of *Dakota Wind*. The artistry of sculptor Pettigrew has been featured in exhibitions and collections throughout the Great Plains and Mountain West.

The choice to donate the sculpture of a Native woman "just felt right," said Phyllis O'Connor. "Look at the statue. One can see by the expression on the face of the woman her feelings of being cold and tired but so proud," Jim O'Connor added.

The plaque on the pedestal reads, "Dakota Wind by Martha Pettigrew. Donated by Phyllis and Jim O'Connor to honor All People Who Have Lived in Wyoming."

GRENVILLE DODGE

Location: Southwest corner of Capitol Avenue and 16ᵗʰ Street
Artist: Guadalupe Barajas
Donors: Kim and Larry Sutherland

Grenville M. Dodge was a man with a one-track mind: he built railroads. Dodge was born in Danvers, Massachusetts, on April 12, 1831. After working his childhood in his father's store and selling produce for a local farm, Dodge graduated from Norwich University in Vermont in 1850 with a degree in civil engineering.

Dodge graduated from Captain Partridge's Military School in 1851 and moved to Peru, Illinois, where he conducted land surveys. By the end of the year, he had found employment with the Illinois Central Railroad and then for the Rock Island Railroad Company. Eventually, he conducted surveys for the Mississippi and Missouri River Railroad that would take him to his future home in Burlington, Iowa.

While working for these railroads, Dodge began contemplating what it would take to build a railroad across the continent. This problem was on the mind of many engineers across the country, as an efficient means

A portrait of General Grenville Dodge. *Wyoming State Archives, Department of State Parks and Cultural Resources.*

was needed to connect the far-off gold fields of California to the rest of the country. In 1853, he began to do reconnaissance west of the Missouri River, looking for a starting point for a transcontinental railroad. During his explorations, he met and was sponsored by Thomas C. Durant, who had strong connections with railroad interests in Iowa and Nebraska.

The outbreak of the Civil War interrupted Dodge's surveys. After several battles, he fought at the Battle of Wilson's Creek and the Battle of Pea Ridge, where he was wounded. Because of his tactics and valor in battle, he was promoted to brigadier general.

Dodge's first command was at Columbus, Kentucky, where he was given the task of rebuilding the badly damaged Mobile and Ohio Railroad. General Ulysses S. Grant then assigned Dodge to command the 2nd Division of the army at Corinth, Mississippi. Following additional battles with Confederate forces, Dodge led his men to his new headquarters in Pulaski, Tennessee, in 1863.

Under the command of William Tecumseh Sherman, Dodge used eight thousand of his men to rebuild the railroad between Decatur and Nashville that had been destroyed by the Rebels. Dodge's men undertook the construction effort without supply, foraging off the land, building their own tools and using any supplies they could capture. In forty days, Dodge's men successfully rebuilt the 102 miles of track by hand. In the course of their work, they had to rebuild 180 bridges. Their most celebrated achievement was the construction of a bridge over the Chattahoochee River that was 14 feet high and 710 feet long in three days. After this success, Dodge accompanied Sherman in his fabled March to the Sea, commanding two divisions. Because of his efforts, Dodge was promoted to major general on May 22, 1864.

Wounded at the Battle of Atlanta, Dodge was given command of the Department of the Missouri while he recovered. He wasted no time, using his command to eliminate remaining guerrilla warfare in the state of Missouri and ending Confederate resistance there. In January 1865, the territories of Kansas, Nebraska and Utah fell under his command. Rising tensions with the plains tribes necessitated that he take direct command of several expeditions in the West to quell the insurrections and defend the transcontinental telegraph and stage lines from attack. He assumed command of all U.S. forces in Dakota and Colorado Territories in July 1865.

While on patrol in the western territories, Dodge rekindled his interest in the transcontinental railroad. He took advantage of his command in engaging the Natives to survey potential routes through the formidable barrier of the Rocky Mountains. He also continued his discussions and reports to Thomas C. Durant, who became the president of the new Union Pacific Railroad following the passage of the Transcontinental Railroad Act of 1862. Through Durant's consultation with Dodge, it was determined to establish the eastern terminus of the Union Pacific railroad in Dodge's hometown of Burlington, Iowa.

With the conclusion of the Civil War in 1865, Dodge became involved with Iowa politics and became the state's senator in 1866 while still a major general in the army. His stint in Congress was short-lived, and he resigned his commission on May 1, 1866. He was immediately hired to be the chief engineer of the Union Pacific Railroad, a position he retained until 1870.

Even before his new appointment, Dodge had poured his efforts into finding the route westward for the Union Pacific. Original plans supported following the Great Platte River Road and the crossing the Continental Divide at South Pass. Dodge and leaders of the Union Pacific rejected that option in favor of a more southerly route, despite its complications. To them, it was vital to get as close to the booming mining center of Denver as possible. Also, if a way could be found to get through the mountains near that point, the federal government would begin paying higher prices to get through the rough terrain hundreds of miles sooner than if the original route was followed. Even better, a southerly route would put the railroad right-of-way near titanic coal deposits that would provide free fuel for the railroad for the foreseeable future.

The Rocky Mountains formed a nearly impossible barrier in establishing the southerly route. Their steep slopes and great depth could not be surmounted unless another pass could be found. Union Pacific surveyors under Dodge's command had already found many potential passes north of Denver, the best being located along the original Overland Trail Route north of Fort Collins or at Lodge Pole Creek in Dakota Territory. There were problems with both options, and Dodge ordered his survey parties to keep looking. Engineer James A. Evans presented another route west of Crow

Grenville Dodge
memorial. *Starley
Talbott photograph.*

Creek in 1865. Upon examining the proposed route, Dodge determined that this new pass would provide the future direction of the railroad's efforts.

From 1866 to 1867, the Union Pacific Railroad made rapid progress across Nebraska, with Dodge spending his time overseeing the route, laying out dozens of new towns and smoothing over any difficulties. When the rails approached a point seventy-five miles west of North Platte, Nebraska, Dodge determined that the time was right to establish a major division point on the banks of Crow Creek. This new facility was vital for the upkeep of the railroad, which relied on powerful yet fragile locomotives to do its work. The new site was almost five hundred miles beyond Omaha, and locomotives that reached this point would have to be extensively repaired before heading farther west across the difficult terrain.

On July 3, 1867, Dodge and his party arrived and began surveying the landscape for the location of a major railroad maintenance and repair

Don Jones, master stonemason, applying cement to the base of the Grenville Dodge statue. *Starley Talbott photograph.*

facility, as well as a community to support it. He named this new community Cheyenne after the fierce tribe that he faced a few years before. He and his men named the streets of the city after the members of their party. Dodge had his own street in town until it was renamed in honor of Francis E. Warren many years later.

As Dodge laid out the town, hundreds of people began to lay claim within the new community in anticipation of the railroad's arrival. By the time Dodge finished his work in late July, the town had grown to more than four hundred people. When the railroad arrived on November 13, the town swelled to a population of nearly ten thousand thanks to the arrival of railroad crews, and it swiftly developed a reputation as one of the worst "Hell on Wheels" towns in history. Dodge was not present for the chaos and was instead engaged with trying to build a bridge across Dale Creek Canyon near the top of Evan's Pass (which he renamed Sherman Pass in honor of the Civil War general and his close friend) and laying out the route beyond.

On May 9, 1869, the Union Pacific Railroad met the Central Pacific Railroad at Promontory Summit in Utah. With the driving of the final spike to complete the transcontinental railroad, Dodge, at age of thirty-eight, had achieved his lifelong dream of building a route across the continent.

Dodge continued to be the chief engineer for the Union Pacific Railroad until 1870. In 1871, he became chief engineer of the California and Texas Railway Construction Company. He toured Europe in 1874 while observing the work on the St. Gotthard Tunnel in Italy and consulting on Russia's Trans-Siberian Railway. Through the 1880s, he oversaw the construction of multiple other railroads in California, Colorado, Iowa, Louisiana, Texas and even Mexico. By the time he finally retired, he had surveyed more than sixty thousand miles of new railroads built during the late nineteenth century.

In a remarkably brief period, the efforts of Grenville Dodge not only completed the first transcontinental railroad in the world but also created the communities of Cheyenne, Laramie, Rawlins and Rock Springs, laying the foundation for the creation of the new state of Wyoming. Whether he ever intended it to be the case, he is the father of our great capital city and the wonderful state of Wyoming that grew from the seeds he sowed at the roof of the continent.

The plaque reads, "Major General Grenville Dodge, Founder of Cheyenne" by Guadalupe Barajas. In tribute to the pioneering spirit of the people of the Capital City of the Old West. A gift of Larry & Kim Sutherland 2022."

DUSTER

Location: Southeast corner of Capitol Avenue and 16th Street
Artist: Bobbie Carlyle
Donor: Leadership Wyoming

The sculpture *Duster* represents the cowboy, an iconic symbol of the West. The statue honors working cowboys throughout Wyoming and other areas. Sculpture artist Bobbie Carlyle envisioned the cowboy as a representative of the first cowboys and cattle ranchers in the area.

The first cattle were brought to Wyoming from Texas in 1866. During the summer and fall of 1867, cattle were driven into the Cheyenne area to

The *Duster* sculpture, honoring cowboys. *Starley Talbott photograph.*

provide meat for the railroad construction crews, the residents of the city and the troops at For D.A. Russell.

"This sculpture brings you back to the past and pays tribute to the cattle barons and cowboys who first brought beef to the railroad towns of the West to be shipped to feed a growing market in the East," said Carlyle.

The high plains around Cheyenne provide arid grassland suitable for stock raising and farming. The cattle industry boomed, and Cheyenne became the cattlemen's headquarters. As the cattle industry boomed, so did Cheyenne, becoming the wealthiest town per capita in the United States by 1884. Some of the most prominent ranch operators included Francis E. Warren and Joseph Carey, two of Wyoming's greatest political leaders.

The glorious years of the millionaire cattle barons came to an end by the end of the 1800s. However, smaller ranchers continued to operate, and the cowboy continues to be a symbol for Wyoming.

Duster was sponsored by the 2010 Class of Leadership Cheyenne, a program of the Greater Cheyenne Chamber of Commerce. Each Leadership Cheyenne Class completes a project to promote the beautification of the Greater Cheyenne area. The sculpture was funded through various fundraising activities in the community.

COMPARING TIME

Location: Northwest Corner of Capitol Avenue and 15ᵗʰ Street
Artist: Joey Bainer
Donor: Jim Ehernberger

A corner facing the Union Pacific Railroad Depot in Cheyenne is a fitting place for a statue of a railroad conductor and a railroad engineer comparing time. In the 1800s, railroads determined their schedules on their own clocks, which could lead to wrecks if each company ran its trains on different times.

On November 18, 1883, individual railroad station clocks were reset as standard time noon was reached within each time zone. Prior to the adoption of standard time, the only time that existed in the United States was local time. This was commonly called "sun time" and was based on the transit of the sun across the meridian. Sun time varied between cities at approximately one minute for every thirteen miles. Many cities adopted a time standard based on local sun time at the city hall or some other designated location. Each railroad adopted the time standard of its home city or some other important city on its lines.

The Union Pacific Railroad operated its trains by at least six different item standards based on sun time at Omaha, Jefferson City, St. Joseph, Denver, Laramie and Salt Lake City. With many different time standards throughout the country, passengers, shippers, railroad officers and employees were confused and bewildered. Mistakes and errors were frequent and sometime disastrous.

Railroad officials convened for several years and adopted a plan for establishing a uniform time standard for all railroads. A notice was issued that all railway clocks governing the operation of trains through the United States be set to the new standard at exactly twelve o'clock noon, Sunday, November 18, 1883. This date was called "the day of two noons." In the eastern part of each time zone there was a "noon" based on sun time.

Left: The *Comparing Time* sculpture, honoring the railroad. *Starley Talbott photograph.*

Opposite: Jim Ehernberger holding a typical railroad watch. *Starley Talbott photograph.*

Therefore, clocks and watches were set back from one to thirty minutes to the new Standard Time so that there was a second "noon" when Standard Time in the community reached twelve o'clock.

It became important for every railroad officer and employee to coordinate their watches and check their watches to make sure that they were operating on the correct time schedule. There was some confusion in the beginning, but Standard Time was gradually accepted throughout the United States.

Safe and efficient movement of trains was accomplished by using timetables, which depends on the use of a consistent time and train crews knowing the precise time. By 1893, the General Railroad Timepiece Standards Commission had presented guidelines to create standards for watches that all railroads were required to follow. Train dispatchers, conductors, enginemen, brakemen, yardmaster and foremen of yard engines were required to equip themselves with approved railway standard watches.

Conductors and enginemen were always to compare their watches before starting on a run or before commencing work each day.

The statue named *Comparing Time* was donated by James "Jim" Ehernberger. Jim loved trains from the time he was a small child. He became a longtime employee of the Union Pacific Railroad and an avid photographer of trains.

Ehernberger was born in Omaha, Nebraska, on July 22, 1937. He lived in Bushnell, Nebraska, for six years and moved to Cheyenne in 1950. Jim spent his free time wandering around the railyards in Cheyenne. He toured the roundhouse, visited the workshop, took photos of trains and made friends with the yardmaster. In May 1953, Jim and other passengers were invited to ride a steam train sponsored by the Rocky Mountain Railroad Club. On the trip, young Ehernberger met other photographers and wanted to be able to shoot photos like the ones they took with cameras that were superior to the simple camera that Jim used.

After returning from the steam train ride, Jim described the camera he wished to own to the yardmaster, who offered to sell him a camera. Since Jim was fifteen years old and had no money to buy a camera, the yardmaster asked Jim if he would like to work for the railroad as a "call boy." Ehernberger celebrated his sixteenth birthday in July and went to work for the Union Pacific, where he worked in several different capacities for thirty-four years.

A plaque on the base of the *Comparing Time* sculpture. *Starley Talbott photograph.*

Jim's job as a "call boy" began at midnight on the days he worked. Many of the railroad workers did not have phones. The caller went to residences or hotels in the downtown area of Cheyenne to let a worker know what shift he would be working. After a month, Jim earned the money to buy a Super D Graflex camera for $250, and he said it was a dream come true.

Ehernberger worked his way through several different positions with the railroad, including train crew dispatcher, assistant in the superintendent's office, private secretary to the superintendent, train dispatcher and assistant manager of operating rules. Then he retired in 1988.

During Jim's years of employment with the railroad, he also took pictures of trains wherever he went. Many of his photographs were published in magazines and books. After retirement, Jim traveled on trains and took photos in South America, Cuba, China, Poland, Germany, Mexico, Guatemala, El Salvador, South Africa and Canada.

Ehernberger has authored and coauthored several magazine articles and books about trains. He is a charter member of the Wyoming State Historical Society, served as a Wyoming State Museum volunteer and served as president of the Rocky Mountain Railroad Club and president of the Union Pacific Historical Society.

HARD TO LEAVE

Location: Northeast corner of Capitol Avenue and 15th Street
Artist: Bobbie Carlyle
Donors: Multiple

The sculpture *Hard to Leave* depicts a cowboy standing in front of the Union Pacific Railroad Depot in Cheyenne. Presumably, the man is getting ready to leave Cheyenne after working on a local ranch. He is looking toward the Wyoming Capitol a few blocks to the north. Perhaps he is finding it hard to leave Cheyenne as he heads off to a new adventure somewhere else.

As history reports, others have also found it hard to leave Cheyenne. Twenty-five-year-old John Feick of Sandusky, Ohio, arrived in Cheyenne on February 2, 1887, to assume his duties supervising the construction of the new capitol building.

Feick wrote the following letter to his wife, Lizzie, in Ohio:

Feby 2, 1887
Dearest Wife!

I just arrived at Cheyenne right side up and handled with care. I tell you it was a long ride. I thought that I went around the world five times, can not tell you any thing about Cheyenne yet, just came in and is very dark, will write you a good long letter tomorrow which you will get Sunday morning if you go to the post office between 9 & 10.

It is snowing & blowing bad enough to scare a man to death the first night, would have written you from Chicago, or Omaha but train went right straight through.

Do not worry about me I will try & do the best I can I feel very lonesome & tired. Yours, John A. Feick

John's next letter to Lizzie came a few days later, as he described his first impressions of Cheyenne:

February 5 1887
Dearest Wife:

I suppose you received the letter I wrote you when I arrived. I had quite a long trip, and feel very lonesome and homesick for you, to be fifteen hundred miles away from you and in a part of the country where you have to wear a belly-band to keep your cap on your head is a pretty bad thing.

There are very wealthy people living in this town but they all look to me like Cow-boys, Lizzie you can not imagine what kind of a country this is you can go just one hundred miles straight out in the country and not see a house or a living sole, but wolves, prarie Dogs, Deer, there are some very heigh mountains that you can see from Cheyenne that have snow on the top all the year around and the cars run to the top of them and that is 8000 feet heigher than Cheyenne. Cheyenne is just two and one half miles heigher in the air than Sandusky is, so you can imagine how the wind blows.

I will close for two night and write you another letter in the morning, hoping to hear from you soon. Your true & faithful husband, John A. Feick

Feick continued to write to Lizzie for more than a year while he worked in Cheyenne. He wrote to her about his work and social activities, and he seemed to adjust to life in the city and even expressed a desire to remain in Cheyenne, as written in his last two letters to Lizzie before leaving.

March 17, 1888
My Dearest Lizzie:

I received your kind & welcome letter this evening and was very glad to hear from you. I am well & glad to hear you are the same, only that I am terrible homesick and anxious to see you all again. I suppose in a week from tonight by this time we will have all our tickets bought and on the train then I will be happy when two days are gone by so as to see Sandusky, but for some reason I hate to leave Cheyenne. I don't know why I am not very much stuck on the town but I hate to leave it.

Mr. Nagle wants me to stay here the worst way & says he will help in every way that he can Mrs. N. sends her best wishes to you...Yours John A.

March 20, 1888
My Dear Lizzie:

I received your letter & was glad to hear from you we are having lots of snow and bad weather, we will all be finished to go home Saturday, if I go

The *Hard to Leave*
statue. *Starley
Talbott photograph.*

*to Salt Lake City you must not be angry with me for I would like to see it
very much if I can work some skeame to get there without George knowing
it. Mrs. Nagle sends her best wishes to you & wishes you were back again.
I will telegraph you when I start for home...Yours John A*

Even though John Feick may have found it hard to leave Cheyenne, family
and duties in Ohio caused him to board the train and return home.

More than one hundred years later, Michael Dixon served as the on-
site architect and historic preservation consultant for the restoration of the
capitol building. Dixon expressed similar thoughts to those of John Feick in
finding Cheyenne hard to leave. Dixon wrote these words in the foreword for
A History Lover's Guide to Cheyenne:

When I arrived in Cheyenne in 2016 to become part of the team for the restoration of the Capitol Building, I was given a box of letters dating from 1887 written by John Feick, mostly to his wife, Lizzie. Feick was the on-site construction supervisor representing his firm Adam Feick & Bros. of Sandusky, Ohio, who had won the contract for constructing the Capitol. He describes his first day in Cheyenne as "snowing and blowing bad enough to scare a man to death." So, I wondered where I really was....I had just arrived after living in the beautiful mountain city of Prizren in the Republic of Kosovo, having spent the past five years in the United States Peace Corps, three of those years in Ukraine (2011–14), then on to Armenia and Kosovo (2015 and 2016). But, as I got further into John Feick's letters, I could relate to his experiences when, eventually, his letters became incredibly positive about Cheyenne, its people and its culture. After over a year on the job, he wrote to Lizzie that "for some reason I hate to leave Cheyenne. I don't know why…but I hate to leave it." I agree with Feick's testament to Cheyenne's hospitality through its gracious people and important historic places.

The sculpture *Hard to Leave* is about choices and opportunities. It was sponsored by multiple people who have found Cheyenne a special place to live.

PART IV

BEYOND CAPITOL
AVENUE

From October 2021 to May 2023, something inspiring happened in Cheyenne. In that brief time, a bronze sculpture was installed on each corner of Capitol Avenue from the Wyoming Capitol on 24th Street to the Union Pacific Train Depot on 15th Street.

The story began as a tiny bud, blossoming like a field of Wyoming wildflowers. Soon, more donors saw the vision inspired by Harvey Deselms, and they began contributing to expand the vision beyond Capitol Avenue.

Deselms's dream included installing statues of animals on 17th Street from the Deselms Fine Arts Gallery on 17th Street and House Avenue to the planned Children's Museum on 17th Street and O'Neil Avenue. Many of the animal sculptures have been installed along 17th Street. Other streets—

Don Jones bringing a statue of a moose across Central Avenue to its location on 17th Street. *Starley Talbott photograph.*

including Carey Avenue, Warren Avenue and Central Avenue—now include numerous bronze sculptures. As of the publication of this book, more than sixty statues have been installed, and many more are planned.

A few of the special animal statues along the 17th Street corridor include the following sculptures.

KITTENS AND CREAM

This sculpture by Robin Laws, on the southwest corner of 17th Street and Warren Avenue, is dedicated to the five generations of the Fogg Family Dairy. They produced milk for Cheyenne's Plains Dairy that no longer exists. The donors include Calvin and Laurell Fogg; Brand, Cheryl and Elijah; Chad and Kate, Hayden, Ryan and Ellen; Kory and Julie, Madeline, Daniel and Kara. 2023.

SPIRITS OF THE OPEN PLAINS

This sculpture by Guadalupe Barajas, on the northwest corner of 17th Street and Central Avenue, was gifted to Cheyenne and Cheyenne Frontier Days™ in memory of Don Kensinger and Arlene Brown Kensinger. The Kensingers are honored for their many dedicated years of service. The donors are Lance, Alice, Teresa, Kim and Curt Theobald. 2022.

THE GUARDIAN

This sculpture by Robin Laws, on the northwest corner of 17th Street and Carey Avenue, honors the women volunteers for Cheyenne Frontier Days™. The statue of a guardian sheepdog honors the life of Marietta Dinneen and other women volunteers. The Wheels group was organized in 1941 to be the guardians of the historic carriages housed in the Old West Museum and featured in the Cheyenne Frontier Days™ parades each year. Marietta Dinneen left a legacy for Cheyenne's history by her contributions to the largest horse-drawn carriage collection in the world. Dinneen, who died at the age of ninety-three in 2023, was an expert in carriage construction and established a database to ensure that the carriage heritage was preserved. Like the guardian sheepdog, the Wheels serve as guardians of the carriages.

SWAT TEAM

Robin Laws was looking out the window of her rural Laramie County home when she saw three of her donkeys huddled together after a rainstorm. The storm had washed away fly repellent, and the donkeys were helping one another out by swatting the flies using their combined tails. The inspiration

Right: The *Kittens and Cream* sculpture on 17th Street. *Starley Talbott photograph.*

Below: The *Spirits of the Open Plains* sculpture, on 17th Street. *Starley Talbott photograph.*

The Guardian sculpture on 17th street. *Starley Talbott photograph.*

The *Swat Team* sculpture on 17th Street. *Starley Talbott photograph.*

led Robin to create this sculpture, on the northeast corner of 17th Street and Thomes Avenue, that she named *Swat Team*. The statue is at a fitting location in front of the Cheyenne Public Safety Center. The statue was donated by Dr. Vic Adoue, DVM, and Linda Trucco-Adoue in honor of the first responders who protect and serve in Cheyenne and Laramie County.

Future sculptures planned for other locations in Cheyenne include:

PRINCESS BLUE WATER
This sculpture by Joey Bainer honors the Native Sioux woman Rose Ecoffey, known by her stage name, Princess Blue Water. Ecoffey was involved with dancing and performing at Cheyenne Frontier Days™ for more than forty years. She brought her children, grandchildren and great-grandchildren to perform at CFD. Her regalia is on display at the CFD Old West Museum in Cheyenne. Donors of the sculpture are Gordon and Beverly Black and Bob and Marirose Morris.

Left: A clay model of *Princess Blue Water*, depicting a Native Sioux woman, shown with the sculptor, Joey Bainer. *Starley Talbott photograph.*

Right: The completed bronze of *Princess Blue Water* before being installed at a permanent location. *Starley Talbott photograph.*

BIBLIOGRAPHY

Adams, Gerald M. "The Air Age Comes to Wyoming." *Annals of Wyoming* 52, no. 2 (1980): 18–29.

Almarcha, Francisco, Trinitario Ferrandez et al. "Symbols, Wolves and Conflicts." *Biological Conservation* 275 (November 2022).

American Oil and Gas Historical Society. "All Pumped Up—Oilfield Technology." aogs.org.

American Public Gas Association. "A Brief History of Natural Gas." apga.org.

Amundson, Michael A. *Wyoming Revisited: Rephotographing the Scenes of Joseph E. Stimson.* Boulder: University Press of Colorado, 2014.

Boeing News 1, no. 8. "Flying for B.A.T." (August 1930): 2–3.

Boeing News 2, no. 2. "Introducing James P. Murray" (February 1931): 1.

Boeing News 2, no. 4. "Veterans of the Mail Service" (April 1931): 2–3.

Burroughs, John Rolfe. *Guardian of the Grasslands: The First Hundred Years of the Wyoming Stock Growers Association.* Cheyenne, WY: Pioneer Printing & Stationary Company, 1971.

Casper Star-Tribune. "Death Claims Senator Francis E. Warren." November 11, 1929, 1.

———. "Jonah Bank Plans Growth." May 11, 2008, 21.

———. "Name of Post Officially Changed to Fort Warren." January 1, 1930, 1.

———. "Warren's Senate Service Was Longest in History." November 11, 1929, 1.

Cheyenne Centennial Committee. *The Magic City of the Plains: Cheyenne 1867–1967.* Cheyenne, WY: self-published, 1967.

Cheyenne Daily Sun-Leader. "Chief Washakie's Funeral." February 28, 1900, p2c2.

———. "Death of Washakie." February 20, 1900, p2c1.

———. "A Great Character: Interesting Incidents in the Life of Chief Washakie." March 12, 1900, p3c2.

———. "Washakie Is Dead." February 20, 1900, p4c3.

Cheyenne State Leader. "Francis McInerney Is Graduated at Annapolis." June 4, 1920, p5c5.

Corliss, Carlton J. *The Day of Two Noons.* Washington, D.C.: Association of American Railroads, 1956.

Cummings, Kathryn Swim. *Esther Hobart Morris*. Glendo, WY: High Plains Press, 2019.

Dennison, Jennifer. "Monuments Man." *Western Horseman Magazine* (November 2021): 66–72.

Dictionary of American Biography. "Washakie." New York: Charles Scribner's Sons, 1998.

Drake, Kerry. "Francis E. Warren: A Massachusetts Farm Boy Who Changed Wyoming." Online Encyclopedia of Wyoming History, November 8, 2014. wyohistory.org.

Ewig, Rick. *Cheyenne: A Sesquicentennial History*. San Antonio, TX: HPN Books, 2017.

———. "Did She Do That?: Examining Esther Morris' Role in the Passage of the Suffrage Act." *Annals of Wyoming* 78, no. 1 (Winter 2006): 26–34.

———. "Give Them What They Want: The Selling of Wyoming's Image Between the World Wars." *Wyoming Almanac: Readings in History*. wyomingalmanac.com.

———. "The Letters of John A. Feick." *Annals of Wyoming* 59, no. 1 (Spring 1987): 2–14.

Field, Sharon Lass, ed. *History of Cheyenne, Wyoming*. Vol. 2, *Laramie County*. Dallas, TX: Curtis Media Corporation, 1989.

Findlay, John. *The Mobilized American West*. Lincoln: University of Nebraska Press, 2023.

Flynn, Shirley. *Let's Go! Let's Show! Let's Rodeo!* Cheyenne, WY: Wigwam Publishing Company, 1996.

Frink, Maurice. *Cow Country Cavalcade: 80 Years of the Wyoming Stock Growers Association*. Denver, CO: Old West Publishing Company, 1954.

Giles, Trevor-Parry, and Marouf A. Hasain Jr. "Necessity or Nine Old Men: The Congressional Debate Over Franklin D. Roosevelt's 1937 Court-Packing Plan." *Rhetorical History of the United States* 7 (2006): 245–78.

Hall of Valor Project. "Francis Xavier McInerney." valor.militarytimes.com.

Harris, Burton. *John Colter: His Years in the Rockies*. Lincoln: University of Nebraska Press, 1993.

Hine, Robert V. *The American West: An Interpretive History*. 2nd ed. Boston, MA: Little, Brown and Company, 1984.

Holsinger, Paul. "Mr. Justice Van Devanter and the New Deal: A Note." *The Historian* 31, no. 1 (November 1968): 57–63.

Houston, Alan Fraser, and Jourdan Moore Houston. "The 1859 Lander Expedition Revisited: 'Worthy Relics' Tell New Tales of a Wind River Wagon Road." *Montana: The Magazine of Western History* 49, no. 2 (Summer 1999): 50.

Kauer, Sarah. "Inspired by the Land: Warren Livestock." Wyoming Stock Growers Land Trust, November 15, 2022, 1–2.

Langland, Tuck. *From Clay to Bronze*. New York: Watson-Guptill Publications, 1999.

Larson, T.A. *History of Wyoming*. Lincoln: University of Nebraska Press, 1963.

Leary, William M. "Billy Mitchell and the Great Transcontinental Air Race of 1919." *Air University Review* 35, no. 4 (May–June 1984): 64–76.

Lightner, Sam, Jr. *Wyoming: A History of the American West*. Lander, WY: Summits and Crux Publishing, 2020.

McCraken, Robert. "Mary O'Hara, in Wyoming, She Found the Grass Green." *Wyoming State Tribune*, May 28, 1952.

Mitra, Steve. *Chicago Tribune*. "Loving Job Pays Off for Golden Apple Winners." March 17, 1992, section 2, 40.

Moulton, Candy. *Roadside History of Wyoming*. Missoula, MT: Mountain Press Publishing Company, 1995.

Navarro, Chris. *Chasing the Wind*. Gaithersburg, MD: Signature Book Printing, 2009.

Neilson, Barry J. "Captain Bonneville." *Annals of Wyoming* 8, no. 4 (April 1932): 608, 610–33.

Noble, Ann Chambers. "The Jonah Field and Pinedale Anticline: A Natural-Gas Success Story." Online Encyclopedia of Wyoming History. wyohistory.org.

Post, Robert. "Willis Van Devanter: Chancellor of the Taft Court." *Journal of Supreme Court History* (November 1, 2020): 287–308.

Reynolds, Sydney. "Chief Washakie: The Redskin Who Saved the White Man's Hide." *American Heritage Magazine* (1960).

Roberts, Phil. "Wyoming Oil: New History of Wyoming." Chapter 10 in *Wyoming Almanac: Readings in History*, 360. wyomingalmanac.com.

Roedel, A.E. "The Mail Must Go." *Annals of Wyoming* 17, no. 1 (Winter 1942): 64.

Rosenberg, Barry, and Catherine Macaulay. *Mavericks of the Sky: The First Daring Pilots of the U.S. Air Mail*. New York: HarperCollins Publishers, 2006.

Scheer, Teva J. *Governor Lady: The Life and Times of Nellie Tayloe Ross*. Columbia: University of Missouri Press, 2005.

Talbott, Starley, and Linda Graves Fabian. *Cheyenne Frontier Days*. Charleston, SC: Arcadia Publishing, 2013.

———. *A History of the Wyoming Capitol*. Charleston, SC: The History Press, 2019.

Talbott, Starley, and Michael E. Kassel. *Historic Lakeview Cemetery of Cheyenne*. Charleston, SC: The History Press, 2023.

———. *A History Lover's Guide to Cheyenne*. Charleston, SC: The History Press, 2021.

———. *Wyoming Airmail Pioneers*. Charleston, SC: The History Press, 2017.

———. *Wyoming's Friendly Skies*. Charleston, SC: The History Press, 2020.

Thompson, D. Claudia. "The Virginian Meets Matt Shepard." *Wyoming Almanac: Readings in History*. wyomingalmanac.com.

Tushnet, Mark. "Willis Van Devanter: The Person." *Journal of Supreme Court History* (November 1, 2020): 308–21.

United States Fish and Wildlife Service. "Gray Wolf." www.fws.gov.

Van Pelt, Lori. *Capital Characters of Old Cheyenne*. Glendo, WY: High Plains Press, 2006.

———. "Cheyenne, Magic City of the Plains." Online Encyclopedia of Wyoming History, October 30, 2017. wyohistory.org.

———. "Willis Van Devanter, Cheyenne Lawyer and U.S. Supreme Court Justice." Online Encyclopedia of Wyoming History, February 14, 2015. wyohistory.org.

Van Zandt, Lieutenant J. Parker. "On the Trail of the Air Mail." *National Geographic Magazine* 49 no. 1 (January 1926): 1–61.

Weidel, Nancy. *Cheyenne: 1867–1917*. Charleston, SC: Arcadia Publishing, 2009.

———. *Sheepwagon: Home on the Range*. Glendo, WY: High Plains Press, 2001.

———. *Wyoming's Historic Ranches*. Charleston, SC: Arcadia Publishing, 2014.

Writers Program of the Works Progress Administration in the State of Wyoming. *Wyoming: A Guide to Its History, Highways and People*. Lincoln: University of Nebraska Press, 1981.

Wyoming Gray Wolf Population Monitoring and Management Annual Report, 2012.

Wyoming State Historical Society, Laramie County Chapter. *Cheyenne Landmarks*. Cheyenne, WY: Pioneer Printing, 1976.

Wyoming State Tribune. "Airship at Park Ready for Flight." March 14, 1911.
————. "Cheyenne to Have Airship of Its Own." January 10, 1911.
————. "Flies 1,000 Feet High at Gillette." July 6, 1911.
————. "Nellie Tayloe Ross Becomes Wyoming's Governor at Noon Monday with Simple Ceremony." January 5, 1925.
————. "School of Aviation." July 4, 1911.
————. "Sheridan Man Hopes to Fly." July 13, 1911.
Wyoming Tribune Eagle. "The Capitol Avenue Bronze Project." June 10, 2023.

Interviews

Bainer, Joey. Personal interview with author Michael Kassel, August 17, 2023, and author Starley Talbott, October 10, 2023.
Barajas, Guadalupe. Personal interview with author Michael E. Kassel, September 17, 2023.
Black, Beverly. Personal interview with author Starley Talbott, November 8, 2023.
Born, Robert. Personal interview with author Starley Talbott, May 5, 2023.
Emerich, Fred, and Keren Meister-Emerich. Personal interview with author Starley Talbott, May 18, 2023.
Jones, Don. Personal interview with author Starley Talbott, May 1, 2023.
Jones-Denkers, Julie. Personal interview with author Starley Talbott, October 10, 2023.
Knapp, Christine. Personal interview with author Starley Talbott, July 17, 2023.
Laws, Robin. Personal interview with author Starley Talbott, September 17, 2023.
Loren, Tanner. Personal interview with author Starley Talbott, August 5, 2022.
Lundeen, George. Personal interview with author Starley Talbott, October 10, 2023.
Pettigrew, Martha. Personal interview with author Starley Talbott, September 23, 2023.
Samuelson, Susan. Personal interview with author Starley Talbott, October 25, 2023.
Trelease, Nathanial. Personal interview with authors Starley Talbott and Michael Kassel, September 23, 2022.

Websites

www.barajasstudio.com.
www.bobbiecarlylesculpture.com.
www.capitolavenuebronze.org.
www.cheyennecity.org.
www.chrisnavarro.com.
www.christineknappsculpture.com.
www.deselmsfineart.com.
www.firstprescheyenne.org.
www.hfjmasonry.com.
www.joelturnerstudio.com.
www.joeybainersculpture.com.
www.juliejonesart.com.
www.lundeensculpture.com.
www.marthapettigrewart.com.
www.railswest.com.
www.richhainesgalleries.com.
www.robinlaws.com.
www.tannerloren.com.
www.wyoarchives.wyo.gov.
www.wyohistory.org.

ABOUT THE AUTHORS

STARLEY TALBOTT has been a freelance author for more than fifty years. She has been published in numerous newspapers and magazine throughout the Rocky Mountain region and is the author of eleven books, including three Arcadia Publishing titles (*Platte County*, *Fort Laramie* and *Cheyenne Frontier Days*) and five titles for The History Press (*Wyoming Airmail Pioneers*, *A History of the Wyoming Capitol*, *Wyoming's Friendly Skies*, *A History Lover's Guide to Cheyenne* and *Historic Lakeview Cemetery of Cheyenne*). Starley holds a BS degree from the University of Wyoming and an MS degree from the University of Nevada. She has lived in several states and foreign countries, loves to travel and has a deep appreciation for history. She is a member of Wyoming Writers, Laramie County Historical Society and the Wyoming State Historical Society.

MICHAEL E. KASSEL serves as the Associate Director and Curator of Collections at the Cheyenne Frontier Days™ Old West Museum. He is an adjunct professor of history at Laramie County Community College in Cheyenne, Wyoming. He holds a BS degree in historic preservation from Southeast Missouri State University, an Associate of the Arts degree in history from Laramie County Community College and a Master of Arts degree from the University of Wyoming. He is the author of *Thunder on High: Cheyenne, Denver and Aviation Supremacy on the Rocky Mountain Front Range*. He is the coauthor of *Wyoming Air Mail Pioneers*, *Wyoming's Friendly Skies*, *A History Lover's Guide to Cheyenne* and *Historic Lakeview Cemetery of Cheyenne* from The History Press.

Visit us at
www.historypress.com